MW01485413

FROM MY

Heart

to

His

A Daily Devotional of Prayers

EMILY A. EDWARDS, PH.D.

LIVING HOPE PUBLISHING

Midland, TX

© 2021 Emily A. Edwards, Ph.D.

All rights reserved. No part of this book may be reproduced in any form or by any electronic or mechanical means, including information storage and retrieval systems, without permission in writing from the publisher, except by a reviewer who may quote brief passages in a review.

Living Hope Publishing

www.LivingHopePublishing.com

Design by ValsyDesigns.com

Scriptures taken from the Holy Bible, New Living Translation, copyright © 1996, 2004, 2007, 2013 by Tyndale House Foundation. Used by permission of Tyndale House Publishers, Inc., Carol Stream, Illinois 60188. All rights reserved.

Scriptures taken from the Holy Bible, New King James version Copyright © 1982 by Thomas Nelson, Inc. Used by Permission. All rights reserved.

Scriptures taken from the Holy Bible, New American Standard Bible. Copyright © The Lockman Foundation 1960, 1962, 1963, 1968, 1971, 1972, 1973, 1975, 1977, 1995. Used by permission. (www.Lockman.org)

Scriptures taken from the Holy Bible, ESV® Bible (The Holy Bible, English Standard Version®) copyright © 2001 by Crossway Bibles, a publishing ministry of Good News Publishers. All rights reserved.

Scriptures taken from the Holy Bible, New International Version®, NIV®. Copyright © 1973, 1978, 1984, 2011 by Biblica, Inc.™ Used by permission of Zondervan. All rights reserved worldwide.

ISBN: 978-0-578-98848-1

Acknowledgements

My gratitude for this book goes to so many people. First, to my Lord and Savior, Jesus Christ, who gave me life and the opportunity to grow in my relationship with him through prayer. To Charles and Frances Younger, whose love and unceasing prayers have helped to sustain me. To Brett and Leah Watkins for their unwavering support and encouragement. To Ben and Bridgette Edwards, whose love has been a rock. To Fred & Valerie Paine, who have been friends, mentors, co-authors, book designers, and encouragers who have lifted me up in daily prayer. To Heidi Tolliver Walker, longtime friend, editor, and mentor who has prayed for and stood by me through many seasons of life. To the many, many others who aren't mentioned but whose support has been invaluable to me over the years. Thank you.

Introduction

Throughout the Bible, we are instructed and encouraged to pray. Yet prayer doesn't mean that our struggles will go away or that our every request will be granted. Rather, when we pray, we are choosing to put our trust in God. Through our prayers, we turn over our concerns and allow him to change the way we deal with our needs and desires.

God always hears our prayers and will give us peace to see us through each challenge. Sometimes, God may not answer our prayers the way we expect. However, we trust that he always has our best interests in mind. We trust that he knows best.

The truth is that intimacy develops as we seek God's face and sit in his presence, spending time in his Word and in prayer.

Many times, "prayer" means that we are running to God and asking him to change our situations. But how often do we sit at his feet, praying, simply to get to know him better? Or learn to trust him more? In the end, those are the times that bear the greatest fruit and utterly transform us.

This isn't to say that it is easy. It's not. Like many others, I have gone through dark times, feeling desperate for answers. During these times, I admit that I'm not looking for spiritual growth. I am looking for peace and comfort. I want to know that everything is going to be okay. I want to find hope in the midst of hopelessness, direction when I feel lost, and rest when I am weary.

The reality is, while some of us experience that peace and comfort in our prayers, not all of us do . . . or not all the time. Sometimes we pray into silence. We wait for answers that are slow in coming. We wonder if God is even listening.

But he is listening, and he yearns to wrap his arms around us and let us fall into his tender care. His heart breaks with every one of our tears that falls. If we persevere in our prayers, the Bible promises that we will find fullness of joy and comfort that no one else can offer, even during times of loneliness and pain.

In these pages, I have turned many of my own prayers into a daily devotional. By no means do I think that these prayers cover the full range of topics for daily prayer. Rather, they are offered as a starting point. It is my desire that they would touch your heart and encourage you in your own prayer life and walk with God. I pray that, through these prayers and your own, you will allow God to draw you into a closer and more intimate relationship with him, always being aware of his abiding love and faithfulness.

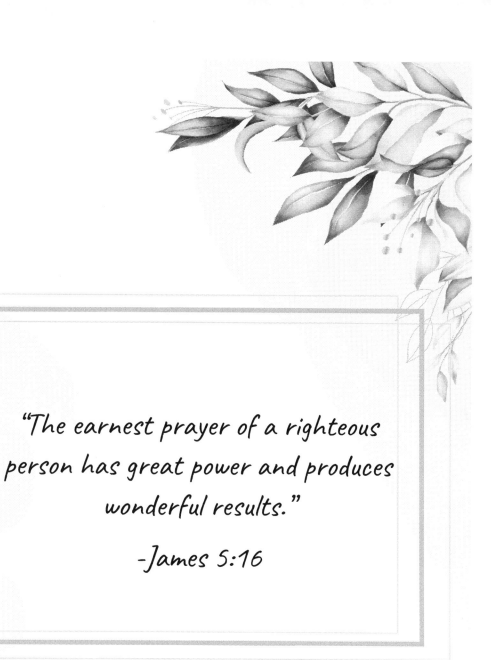

"The earnest prayer of a righteous person has great power and produces wonderful results."

-James 5:16

Day 1

Prayer of Thanksgiving for the Day

Dear Jesus,

The beauty of a new day encourages my heart. You have given me the precious gift of life. This is the day you have made. I will rejoice and be glad in it. To you, I submit this day and all that is in it. I choose to praise you throughout the day, and I pray that I would not take even a moment for granted. My life belongs to you, and each day, you have a plan. I invite you to lead me through whatever your plan is for me today.

Help me look with appreciation upon this day. Your creation is superb. How you paint the beauty of a sunrise, cloak the ground with white, and enable flowers to bloom is beyond my understanding. I am in awe of your creation.

Thank you for the grace and mercy you have shown to me and others. Your love is above all things. There is nothing in this life that can tear me away from you. You have me in the palm of your hand and will not let me go.

You are my God, and I love you. Through the day, I will walk with you as I experience the life you've given me. You have much to show me, and I will learn from you. I will follow closely and listen for your voice.

In your name I pray, amen.

"This is the day that the Lord has made; let us rejoice and be glad in it" (Psalm 118:24).

Journal Your Thoughts

Day 2

Prayer for Opportunities in the Day

Dear Lord,

Thank you that each day is filled with opportunities. I pray that I would see with spiritual eyes what you are calling me to do today. When you speak, help me to do more than hear. I want your Holy Spirit to move me to action. I pray that each experience would teach me more about you. That is worth more than gold.

You also have a plan for those whom you put in my path today. May I have a servant's heart and encourage each one along the journey. If someone needs help, Lord, guide me in how I should respond. Give me the wisdom and willingness to act in a way that represents you.

I pray for the Church, your body, that we would claim the inheritance of the kingdom and walk by faith and not fear. There are many dark alleys in this world, and you provide your light to drive away the darkness. Satan cannot bear your light, and he will cower from your presence through us.

I pray for your kingdom to expand and for the workers to answer the call. My heart is ready. Whom could I encourage to join in the harvest? May the value of this call fill our hearts so that there is no misunderstanding about from whom it is coming. To you, God, goes all the glory.

In Jesus' name, amen.

"So encourage each other and build each other up, just as you are already doing" (1 Thessalonians 5:11).

Journal Your Thoughts

Day 3

Prayer for a Sensitive and Compassionate Heart

Dear Almighty God,

You are so good at knowing what each of us needs and for providing for those needs, whether they are physical, financial, spiritual, or emotional. I pray for the same sensitive and compassionate heart towards those around me.

Help me to actively listen so that I can perceive when someone is in need. Help me to look into others' eyes as they speak. Help me to quiet my thoughts so that I can give my full attention to their words. Help me to ask clarifying questions so I can find out what is on their hearts. Thank you for showing me how to care for others and be aware of their needs.

When I see others who are hurting, help me know how to comfort them. As I hear the cries of their hearts, help me understand and speak with empathy. May I do more than acknowledge the person's need. May my words translate into action. If someone is weighed down with burdens, give me a willing heart to help them carry those burdens to you.

Jesus, you have demonstrated all of these things for us and much more. That is how we learn to be sensitive and compassionate to the needs of others—by observing the way you have been sensitive and compassionate to us. I praise you for your wonderful gift of grace and mercy.

In Jesus' name I pray, amen.

"All praise to God, the Father of our Lord Jesus Christ. God is our merciful Father and the source of all comfort. He comforts us in all our troubles so that we can comfort

others. When they are troubled, we will be able to give
them the same comfort God has given us"
(2 Corinthians 1:3-4).

Journal Your Thoughts

Day 4

Prayer to Seek First His Kingdom

Dear Lord,

There are so many directions in life that I can turn. With every move I make, the world tempts me, and sometimes it is hard to resist its call. I confess that I seek what I desire rather than your desire for me. At times, I accept less than what you have planned for me. Convict and change my heart to turn to you alone.

I pray to be part of a community that seeks you in all things and that does not depend solely on the spiritual gifts or willingness of individual people. Your plan is greater than anything I or anyone else can create—or hinder. Encourage me to seek your guidance so that I and others in the Church can be fruitful.

Lord, let me see and understand what you want me to do for you, and I will do it. I desire your will and not mine. I desire to see your hand move in my life; empower me to be your hands and feet. Right action is founded upon seeking you with my heart and soul.

Allow me, Lord, to encourage others to seek your face in all things, as well. I pray that they would find true peace and contentment in doing so, and that I would find my peace and contentment in these things, as well.

In your name I pray, amen.

"Trust in the Lord with all your heart, and lean not on your own understanding; in all your ways acknowledge him, and he shall direct your paths" (Proverbs 3:5-6).

Journal Your Thoughts

Day 5

Prayer for Joy

Dear Lord,

You tell us to consider it all joy when we experience difficulties and trials. If we are called to experience joy, even when our hearts are hurting, this shows us that joy means much more than being happy. It is a deep choice that we make that reflects what we truly believe.

Joy is internal, while happiness is external. Joy is independent of circumstances, while happiness is dependent on them. Please remind me that true joy comes from believing in and trusting Jesus Christ, and nothing can take away that type of joy. Thank you that Jesus holds me in the palm of his hand and will never let me go.

Holy Spirit, the joy I express from my core is from you. Your Spirit joins with my spirit to reveal your truth. Truth shows us the way to go, and no matter what happens, I can truly be joyful because of Jesus.

I pray for those who do not know your joy. They live day to day, perhaps looking for joy from the world and all it has to offer. They find this does not last, but in contrast, your joy, Lord, lasts for eternity.

I pray specifically for those who haven't felt joyous in a long time. Allow them to feel your presence, dear Jesus. They need you more than ever. Only you can breathe new life into every hurting heart. Your joy is there for all who accept it. I pray that all who are hurting would accept this gift.

In your name I pray, amen.

"Dear brothers and sisters, when troubles of any kind come your way, consider it an opportunity for great joy. For you know that when your faith is tested, your endurance has a chance to grow. So let it grow, for when

your endurance is fully developed, you will be perfect and complete, needing nothing" (James 1:2-4).

Journal Your Thoughts

Day 6

Prayer for Peace

Dear Jesus,

Thank you for being the Prince of Peace. Your peace is a wonderful gift that you give me. You are the creator of peace, and in unexplainable ways, your peace can be felt even during the worst chaos. I pray for peace in this world. For your glory, I pray for peace in specific areas of people's lives.

I pray for peace in the lives of those who are struggling with confusion, anxiety, and frustration. Their hearts are breaking, Father, and I lift them up to you for healing. I pray that they would feel your arms of love around them and know how deeply you care for them.

I pray for peace in my own life. There are times when life becomes so messy that I don't know which way to turn. I feel alone and abandoned. Anxiety comes upon me, and it is hard to think clearly.

I plead for your peace. I desire your strength to keep running the race you have put before me. You are the goal, and I have victory because of you. I can reach the finish line because you empower me and cheer me on to victory.

In Jesus' name I pray, amen.

"I am leaving you with a gift—peace of mind and heart. And the peace I give is a gift the world cannot give. So don't be troubled or afraid" (John 14:27).

Journal Your Thoughts

Day 1

Prayer for Evidence of the Fruit of the Spirit

Dear Lord,

You have given me the fruit of your Spirit: love, joy, peace, patience, kindness, goodness, faithfulness, gentleness, and self-control. Thank you for each of these gifts, and I pray that they would be evident in my life.

It is my choice to apply each fruit—a special gift with a special purpose—each day. Even on the days when I feel down or am struggling, I pray that I would choose the fruit of the Spirit over my fickle emotions. I pray that I would experience love, joy, and peace. Enable me to be patient, kind, good, faithful, and gentle. Help me to exercise self-control.

These qualities are important because when I walk in them, I am reflecting you. May others see that I belong to you and not to the world. Help me choose to show your fruit rather than my connection to the world. The world cares little about the gifts of the Spirit, but promotes everything that is in opposition to them. Thank you for first modeling these gifts so that we know how to walk in them, too.

Your Spirit is so beautiful. I want to show the fruit of your Spirit in all my relationships. At times, it seems so difficult, but you will help me. You love me so much, and you want me to be an encouragement. I know your Spirit will be there with me and empower me, if I choose to listen.

In your precious name I pray, amen.

"But the Holy Spirit produces this kind of fruit in our lives: love, joy, peace, patience, kindness, goodness, faithfulness, gentleness, and self-control. There is no law against these things! Those who belong to Christ Jesus

have nailed the passions and desires of their sinful nature to his cross and crucified them there. Since we are living by the Spirit, let us follow the Spirit's leading in every part of our lives" (Gal. 5:22-25).

Journal Your Thoughts

_____

_____

_____

_____

_____

_____

_____

_____

_____

_____

_____

_____

_____

_____

_____

_____

_____

_____

_____

Day 8

Prayer for Healing from the Inside Out

Dear Precious Lord,

The tragedies of life can leave scars on our souls and affect us in ways we don't even realize. I pray against any negative reactions to scarring that may occur in the lives of people today. So many are hurting. I pray for healing in their souls and that they would be able to walk in freedom, even in the midst of troubled times. I pray that your Holy Spirit would take the reins of their lives so that they can be transformed into the people you desire them to be.

It is your Word that transforms us and changes us from the inside out, so I pray for a passion for Scripture. Like the deer that pants for water, I want to hunger and thirst to pick up the Bible and drink in the living water. I pray that I would let go of old fleshly patterns that do me harm and replace them with new ones that you have designed.

Lord, my life is so much better when I follow your ways and seek your face. Obedience will help me in the process of transformation. I choose to come into your presence so that I can experience your work in my heart.

May you be glorified by my prayer.

In your name, amen.

"My child, pay attention to what I say. Listen carefully to my words. Don't lose sight of them. Let them penetrate deep into your heart, for they bring life to those who find them, and healing to their whole body" (Prov. 4:20–22).

Journal Your Thoughts

Day 9

Prayer to Turn Away from Evil

Dear Abba, Father,

I pray for your strength to turn away from evil when it comes into my presence. The choices I make are either for good or evil, for the Spirit or the flesh. I want to make the consistent choice to honor you.

Evil seems to lurk everywhere, and it constantly tries to trip me up. The wisdom I need comes from you. I must daily take in your Word and memorize the Scriptures I need for when sin taunts me. Help me never to turn my back on you.

Jesus, I pray for those who are not following you right now. I pray that their spiritual eyes would be opened so that they could see that they are living the wrong way. Give them the wisdom, courage, and strength to shun evil and choose the right path. I know you love them dearly, Lord.

Protect my heart, O Lord, and forgive me for the times I've been weak and given the evil one a foothold in my life. It's tempting to become angry and bitter and lose my focus on you. This is destructive to my relationship with you, and I want to be close to you always. Keep me in the palm of your hand.

In Jesus' name I pray, amen.

"I have hidden your word in my heart, that I might not sin against you" (Psalm 119:11).

Journal Your Thoughts

Day 10

Prayer for Repentance

Dear God of Righteousness,

I have said and done things that go against your Word, and nothing I have done is hidden from you. I repent and ask for forgiveness. I pray that my heart would be set right with you once again. If I have fallen into a pattern of making wrong choices, I want to break that cycle and live as a model of repentant living.

Break my heart, Lord, for what breaks yours. I pray for eyes to see your truth in these matters, especially when the choice between good and evil is plain. I desire your wisdom, and I know you are a God who gives generously to his children.

I no longer need to be imprisoned by my sin, for you always provide me with a way out. Thank you, Jesus, for this promise. Your Holy Spirit can guide me out of my jail cell, just as you guided Peter out of his.

Help me to listen, accept, and obey what you are telling me. I know you will never force your will onto me; I must receive it. I can trust that you always have my best interest at heart. Your way is the best way. My way leads to death, while yours leads to life. I want to follow you.

In Jesus' name I pray, amen.

"Now repent of your sins and turn to God, so that your sins may be wiped away. Then times of refreshment will come from the presence of the Lord, and he will again send you Jesus, your appointed Messiah" (Acts 3:19–20).

Journal Your Thoughts

Day 11

Prayer Against Sin

Dear Abba, Father,

Sin came to our world with the first bite of the forbidden fruit. It wasn't your plan for mankind to live with a sinful nature, but that is what we chose. Please help me resist sin in my life every day. My only hope for this is you. Even when I fall, you will be there to pick me up again.

We are all born into a sinful nature and vulnerable to the enemy. Sometimes it's hard for me not to assign levels of sin to people who do wrong. Yet I know that in your eyes, sin is sin. Even my "little white lies" are sin.

I want to pray for people to have freedom from any sins that are keeping them imprisoned. Lord, please help them break the chains and become free people who live in victory for you.

I praise and thank you for giving me a way—submission to your will—as described in your Word. This is the path to standing up under the burden of sin. No matter how great the temptation, you promise that there will always be a way of escape. Thank you, Father, for this promise. I know that I am not hopeless, but I have hope in you to resist temptation.

In Jesus' name I pray, amen.

"The temptations in your life are no different from what others experience. And God is faithful. He will not allow the temptation to be more than you can stand. When you are tempted, he will show you a way out so that you can endure" (1 Cor. 10:13).

Journal Your Thoughts

Day 12

Prayer for Knowing My Identity in Christ

Dear Lord,

The messages of the world try to communicate to me who I am or who I should be. But the world has no say in who I am because the world did not create me. You did, and the only one who has the right to say who I am is you. You tell me that I am your child and that I am deeply loved. You tell me that I am adopted by you and that you chose me. You give me other wonderful promises, too.

Lord, may I focus more on my true identity than on anyone or anything else. It is the one sure thing I can hold on to. My life is a reflection of your love. Thank you that your light is in me and radiates in the darkness of troubled times.

I pray for people who are struggling with their identities. I pray that you would confirm how important they are to you. Reveal to their hearts the infinite value you place on them and that their worth can never be diminished. Let them realize that they have a true purpose, and it is identified in you.

Thank you that each person you create has high value. You created mankind in your image—we are yours!

In Jesus' name I pray, amen.

"Because we are his children, God has sent the Spirit of his Son into our hearts, prompting us to call out, 'Abba, Father.' Now you are no longer a slave but God's own child. And since you are his child, God has made you his heir" (Gal. 4:6-7).

Journal Your Thoughts

Day 13

Prayer to Experience Abundant Life

Dear Jesus,

You promise that my life can be abundant in you. I pray that you would show me how to live an abundant life. I know that this is not a promise that we will be wealthy or live in mansions or have thousands of friends. "Abundant life" means that you promise us peace, joy, and purpose. It means that when we live according to your will, our lives will be characterized by your blessings. There is nothing better than the richness of the blessings you provide.

While abundance does not mean earthly things, you delight in giving good gifts to your children. Thank you for providing for me and giving me more than I need or deserve. I'm grateful that you share your life with me, walk with me, and guide me each day. The richness of having fellowship with you, O God, and with your people makes me feel wealthy beyond measure. The Spirit who connects me to you and others also brings me joy and peace beyond understanding.

I pray that those who seem to lack joy and peace would experience your abundant life and share it with others. I pray for their healing and restoration.

I pray that my abundant life would be one that reflects you. I desire your light to shine through me at all times. This can be if I keep my eyes on you. Draw me close to you, dear Jesus.

In your name I pray, amen.

"The thief's purpose is to steal and kill and destroy.
My purpose is to give them a rich and satisfying life"
(John 10:10).

Journal Your Thoughts

Day 14

Prayer to Trust God with All My Heart

Dear God,

Trust is a tough thing. The wounds that I carry in my heart lead me to doubt rather than trust. When I trust, I feel that I am being set up for a fall. I pray, Lord, that the hurt in my soul caused by _____ would be healed so that I can trust again. Being free to trust you completely will bring me to another level in experiencing the abundant life you have for me.

You are my protector and keeper. Thank you that you have never let me down. You are always faithful. I can count on you to bring me safely through the deep waters of life. To fully trust and allow you in all areas of my heart, I must let go of the things that clutter my spirit and bring me fear and unrest. Fear was never your plan for me. My sinful nature sometimes takes on the things of this world, which include mistrust in you.

Today I choose to take steps to trust you. Whenever I begin to feel fearful or stressed, I will redirect each thought to the cross. You have taken care of all those burdens, and I don't need to hold on to them. Thank you, Lord Jesus!

In your name I pray, amen.

"When you go through deep waters, I will be with you. When you go through rivers of difficulty, you will not drown. When you walk through the fire of oppression, you will not be burned up; the flames will not consume you. For I am the Lord, your God, the Holy One of Israel, your Savior. I gave Egypt as a ransom for your freedom; I gave Ethiopia and Seba in your place" (Isa. 43:2–3).

Journal Your Thoughts

Day 15

Prayer for Humility

Dear Heavenly Father,

Thank you for your example of humility shown through the life of Jesus. I pray for the strength to follow his example, thinking of others before myself and looking out for the interests of others.

I confess that being humble is hard for me, especially when I want to be recognized for something I have said or done. It's so easy for me to want to take the glory. Doing so is arrogance, and it is sin. I repent. You deserve all the praise and glory, and it is for my benefit that the glory is directed to you. You are worthy of it all. It reminds me that when I see you at work, I am to praise you in reverence.

I am your servant, Lord. Whatever happens through me is your work. I love the way you invite me to serve with you. My life is so much better when I humbly fall at your feet, ready to pour your love back out. When I make excuses, I am showing the sin of pride that keeps me from you. I repent of that selfishness.

I pray for a humble heart. Mold me and conform me into the image of your Son, Jesus. My hands are open to you.

In Jesus' name I pray, amen.

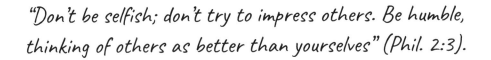

"Don't be selfish; don't try to impress others. Be humble, thinking of others as better than yourselves" (Phil. 2:3).

Journal Your Thoughts

Day 16

Prayer for Revival to Seek God

Dear Father God,

Revival is a renewing of my passion for you. I want to drink deeply of your Spirit today. When I am spiritually dry, I need your Spirit to flood over me. Your living water brings life to the dead things in me and flushes away all that needs to be cleansed. Once my soul is renewed, I can experience new life like never before.

How lovely everything is when I look through the eyes of revival! Your creation seems more vibrant, and I feel more alive. Who but you could be the author of such wonderful things? The world offers chaos; you offer peace. The fire that burns in me is your Spirit, who declares to my utmost being who you are—Truth.

In response, what do I declare? You are Lord! I pray that I would always boldly declare who you are both before men and before you. You are God alone. As I declare that truth boldly, I pray that others would see your flames burning in me.

I pray for revival in our land. We are lost and looking for something that will satisfy. Unless it is you, what we choose will dissolve into nothing. You are the only one who satisfies. Thank you for your never-ending gift of new life.

In Jesus' name I pray, amen.

"In those days when you pray, I will listen. If you look for me wholeheartedly, you will find me" (Jer. 29:12–13).

Journal Your Thoughts

Day 17

Prayer for Revival of a Passion for God's Word

Dear Jesus,

The book of John tells me that in the beginning, there was the Word. Your Word is, and always was. It has always been, breathing life into being. It is the bread that I eat each day. You provide me with this food, Lord, and I pray that my heart would be thankful for each spiritual meal that you feed me.

I pray for a revival of passion for your Word in me. I lift up those who don't want to listen, who shun your Word, or who would rather hear a word that connects to what they desire than to what pleases you. Lord, I ask that you grasp their hearts. Nudge their spirits and point them to your great love for them.

You can heal this land, O Lord, and that is your desire. I ask you to do a work in your people that will expand your kingdom. Help me to encourage others to lay down their desires and seek yours. Thank you that your longings for us can be found in your Word. You do not keep your will a secret. You tell us of your longings and plans with love.

I pray all these things in your precious and holy name, amen.

"Oh, the joys of those who do not follow the advice of the wicked, or stand around with sinners, or join in with mockers. But they delight in the law of the Lord, meditating on it day and night. They are like trees planted along the riverbank, bearing fruit each season. Their

leaves never wither, and they prosper in all they do"
(Psalm 1:1-3).

Journal Your Thoughts

_____
_____
_____
_____
_____
_____
_____
_____
_____
_____
_____
_____
_____
_____
_____
_____
_____
_____

Day 18

Prayer of Thankfulness

Dear Awesome God,

Thank you for creating me and giving me life. Thank you that you have given me salvation. I praise you for the unique gifts with which you have entrusted me, and I pray that I would always use them to bring you praise.

My lips long to praise and thank you for the changes you have made in my life. Because of you, I experience peace and contentment, even when my world seems chaotic. I can lift up my hands and heart to you, and your Spirit will help me soar above earthly things.

Who am I that you even think about me? I cannot imagine my importance to you. You are intentional in showing your love for me. The provision I have, the people who surround me, and the Word you have given are all reflections of your great love and mercy.

Thank you for loving me in real ways. I praise you for who you are and what you mean to me.

In Jesus' name I pray, amen.

"Give thanks to the Lord, for he is good! His faithful love endures forever" (Psalm 107:1).

Journal Your Thoughts

Day 19

Prayer for Living Wholeheartedly for God

Dear Everlasting God,

I want to live fully for you. I believe that living unreservedly for you will allow me to be released from any chains of sin that hold me down. I pray for release from all spiritual shackles that keep me from the freedom you intend for me. Break down any walls of sin that keep me from you.

Lord, I repent and ask you to free me from transgressions. I want to be in agreement with you regarding my sin. Help me to discern what I must release and what I must hold on to. I don't want to be lukewarm in my faith. I want to be on fire, passionate, and intentional about knowing you and serving you with all I have to offer.

Take away my desire for things that distract me, Father God, so that I no longer want them in my life. I want to run the race for you and finish well.

You want to set me free. Today and every day, I choose your freedom.

In Jesus' name I pray, amen.

"I don't mean to say that I have already achieved these things or that I have already reached perfection. But I press on to possess that perfection for which Christ Jesus first possessed me. No, dear brothers and sisters, I have not achieved it, but I focus on this one thing: Forgetting the past and looking forward to what lies ahead, I press on to reach the end of the race and receive the heavenly

prize for which God, through Christ Jesus, is calling us"
(Phil. 3:12–14).

Journal Your Thoughts

_____
_____
_____
_____
_____
_____
_____
_____
_____
_____
_____
_____
_____
_____
_____
_____
_____
_____
_____

Day 20

Prayer for Greater Faith in God

Dear Everlasting God,

You are always faithful. In comparison to your great faithfulness, my faith is so small. Jesus, you said that if I have the faith of a mustard seed, I can move mountains. I'm grateful for that promise because sometimes that seed of faith is all I have. Thank you that it is enough to allow me to stand when everything else is falling apart.

Faith is believing what I can't see. Although I don't see you with my physical eyes, Jesus, I know that you are a very present help. I pray that my faith would be strengthened by the experiences I have with you. The challenges in my life are opportunities for my faith to grow, so thank you for those difficulties that shape and mold me.

Distractions can take my eyes off you if I let them. During those times when I can't see you and I feel alone, please remind me of your constant care for me. Give me the inner strength to overcome troubles and temptations and stay focused on you. That is when my faith will grow. That is when I will achieve victory.

Thank you, Lord!

In your name I pray, amen.

"So be truly glad. There is wonderful joy ahead, even though you must endure many trials for a little while. These trials will show that your faith is genuine. It is being tested as fire tests and purifies gold—though your faith is far more precious than mere gold. So when your faith remains strong through many trials, it will bring you

much praise and glory and honor on the day when Jesus Christ is revealed to the whole world" (1 Pet. 1:6–7).

Journal Your Thoughts

_____

_____

_____

_____

_____

_____

_____

_____

_____

_____

_____

_____

_____

_____

_____

_____

_____

_____

_____

_____

Day 21

Prayer Against a Bad Attitude

Dear Precious Lord,

Sometimes it seems as if everything in my life is going wrong. When that happens, I let my attitude go south, too. This only makes matters worse and keeps me from shining the light of Jesus. I pray that my words and actions, along with my attitude, would always reflect your great love and mercy.

I realize that I am in a world filled with darkness, and sometimes that darkness seems to overwhelm me. But Lord, I pray that you would let me see the light of your hope and shine that light brightly for those around me. There is hope in the midst of all things because of you.

I pray, Lord, for people who are facing difficulties and whose attitudes are suffering. They need to see your resurrection power. They need to know that you have not left them. I pray that you would use me and other believers to boost their confidence. I pray that they would receive new outlooks from you so that they can stand strong when the winds of adversity blow.

Hold us close to you, dear Lord. We are precious in your sight, and you know exactly what we need.

In Jesus' name I pray, amen.

"Yet I still dare to hope when I remember this: The faithful love of the Lord never ends! His mercies never cease. Great is his faithfulness; his mercies begin afresh each morning. I say to myself, 'The Lord is my inheritance; therefore, I will hope in him!' The Lord is good to those who depend on him, to those who search for

him. So it is good to wait quietly for salvation from the Lord" (Lam. 3:21–26).

Journal Your Thoughts

_____
_____
_____
_____
_____
_____
_____
_____
_____
_____
_____
_____
_____
_____
_____
_____
_____
_____
_____

Day 22

Prayer Not to Stray from God

Dear Lord,

You have been faithful from the beginning of time. No matter how far I stray, you are loving, forgiving, and want me to return to you. You have protected me and provided for me each day. Why is it that I can easily slide away from you when worldly things distract me? It seems that when things are going well, my faith starts to falter as if I have no need for you. Forgive me, dear Lord.

Please give me a greater faith in you. I want a faith that can stand up to anything. That kind of faith is mine for the taking, but I need to choose to lean on that faith and exercise it. You have said in your Word that faith the size of a mustard seed will move mountains. Is my faith even that big? Can it be detected?

I pray for those whose faith has been challenged by life's circumstances. I pray that they would stand strong and not let go. You are holding on to them. I pray that you would give them a miracle through this challenge. Amen.

"It is impossible to please God without faith. Anyone who wants to come to him must believe that God exists and that he rewards those who sincerely seek him"
(Heb. 11:6).

Journal Your Thoughts

Day 23

Prayer of Praise and Thanksgiving

Dear Lord,

How awesome are your ways. My mind cannot fully comprehend all that you do and all that you are. As I look out over the waters, I cannot see the other side, but you can. You, O Lord, created it all. As the sunshine sprinkles beauty over the waters, so your love sparkles as it shines on me. You are in control of every movement.

It is wonderful to know whom to thank for all the beauty in the world. It is what you alone have done. If you were not so wonderful, so incomprehensible, human beings might become prideful and take credit for your work. I pray that I never claim responsibility for what you have done.

If I took from morning to night to consider all the ways you have blessed me, there would not be enough time to list them all. There are so many seen and unseen blessings that I cannot fully fathom them all. That is why I need to listen to your voice carefully. Thank you, Lord, for never slumbering and always being attentive to me.

I lift up my hands to you, God, for you are worthy of my praise. I am so grateful for all the things you do in my life.

In Jesus' name I pray, amen.

"Enter his gates with thanksgiving; go into his courts with praise. Give thanks to him and praise his name" (Psalm 100:4).

Journal Your Thoughts

Day 24

Prayer for Living Fully for God

Dear Abba, Father,

How many times have I given you the leftovers of my life? You deserve so much more than a sliver of my time, energy, finances, and more. Not only are you worthy, but also you promise blessing upon blessing on whatever I give to you from the heart. I cannot out-give you, ever.

I know that I am not the only one who struggles with giving you all I am, so I also pray for those who look to the world first and you second … or third. I pray that we would encourage one another to live fully for you and keep each other accountable. There are so many demands on our lives that we are so easily distracted from our purpose. Instead of trying to stay busy all the time, we accomplish so much more by taking the time now and then to simply be still and drink in your wisdom.

First thing every morning, help me make a commitment to keep you number one throughout the day. When temptations arise, use your Holy Spirit to remind me of my promise to you and be strengthened to live it out. I'm excited to get started, knowing that you will help me and show me things I can't imagine.

I pray all these things in Jesus' name, amen!

"Seek the Kingdom of God above all else, and live righteously, and he will give you everything you need"
(Matt. 6:33).

Journal Your Thoughts

Day 25

Prayer for Stronger Faith in God

Dear Lord,

You have been faithful since the day I was born. No matter how far I have strayed, you have forgiven me, loved me, and desperately wanted me to return to you. You have protected me and provided for me each day. Why is it that I can so easily slide away from you when worldly things distract me? It seems that when things are good in my life, my faith starts to falter as if I have no need for you. Forgive me, dear Lord.

Please give me a stronger faith that can withstand the enemy's attacks. I want a faith that can stand up to anything this world can throw at me. That kind of faith is mine for the taking, but I need to choose to walk in it. I think about David going against Goliath. David had fear, but his faith was stronger. How strong is my faith? Is it stronger than my fear?

I pray for those whose faith has been weakened by the battering that life often gives. I pray that they would stand strong and not waiver. You are holding on to them. I pray that you would send a miracle to help them in the midst of their challenges.

In your name I pray, amen.

"It is impossible to please God without faith. Anyone who wants to come to him must believe that God exists and that he rewards those who sincerely seek him"
(Heb. 11:6).

Journal Your Thoughts

Day 26

Prayer for a New Attitude

Dear Lord,

Like the rudder of a ship, my attitude determines my direction. It affects all that I say and do. I repent of the times I have allowed my emotions and circumstances to get in the way so that my attitude has not reflected you. Forgive me. I pray that I would submit all that I am to your Holy Spirit so that I might have the best attitude at all times. When I get down, help me to rely on your promises to lift me up again. It's a choice that I make, and you empower it.

Having a good attitude is difficult when life is hard. It's easy to see no hope. If I believe that life's circumstances are the end of the story, then my attitude becomes a prison cell. But my circumstances are not the end of my story. In you, all things are possible. You are the key that frees me from imprisonment. I pray that my attitude would not reflect my feelings and emotions, but what I know to be true.

I pray for those who need an attitude adjustment. Lord, you did not create us to have bad attitudes, so I pray your grace and mercy over them so they could see your goodness in all areas of their lives. I pray that their eyes would be focused on you and not their circumstances. Their individual situations may change, but you will never change. You are the same yesterday, today, and forever.

My attitude rests on your power and strength. You are the one who created me, so you are the one who can judge my attitude. You want me to have a good outlook and be positive. Through you, I can do this.

I pray these things in your name, amen.

"Do everything without complaining and arguing, so that no one can criticize you. Live clean, innocent lives as

children of God, shining like bright lights in a world full of crooked and perverse people" (Phil. 2:14–15).

Journal Your Thoughts

Day 27

Prayer for a Renewed Mind

Dear Heavenly Father,

Newness comes out of death. A seed must die before it can start to grow. So it is with things in my mind that are not of you. They, too, need to die. They must die to make room for the more valuable thoughts and experiences that you want to give me. What you have is better than what the world offers.

Lord, I pray that I would make the choice every day to renew my mind. I want to flush out the bad and pour in your good. In a state of renewal, I feel recreated. But I cannot do this on my own. It is only through your hand. For renewal to occur, my mind must be focused on you and your goodness and not on things of this world.

There is so much pain around me. Instead of dwelling on that pain, help me to see it through your eyes. Rather than becoming bitter and pointing fingers, you invite me to join you in your works. I must listen carefully and obey. If I resist, I will lose the blessing of seeing what you will do through me.

Oftentimes, I feel inadequate. The tasks that you set before me seem too big for me to handle. The truth is that they *are* too big for me to handle, but you are not asking me to take on these challenges alone. You are with me. You will strengthen and empower me to do what you have called me to do.

In the name of Jesus, I pray, amen.

"Don't copy the behavior and customs of this world, but let God transform you into a new person by changing the way you think. Then you will learn to know God's will for you, which is good and pleasing and perfect" (Rom. 12:2).

Journal Your Thoughts

Day 28

Prayer for Digging Deeper into God's Word

Dear King of Kings,

I want to know more about you and have a more intimate relationship with you. One way I can do this is by reading the Bible. Your Word teaches and equips me to be the best I can be. It teaches me to reflect who you are.

I pray that I would be obedient in what you have called me to do. May I not be slothful in the way I handle that which you have put before me. Instruct and teach me. Give me discernment and wisdom as I read your Word. When I fall short, give me understanding where growth is needed.

Whether it is as soon as I wake up in the morning, at some point throughout the day, or before I go to bed, help me to take the time to dig deeper into your Word. Thank you for the people you have put in my path to help me grow spiritually. Let us encourage one another on this journey and build deep and meaningful relationships. I pray blessings on those you put around me and on their time in the Word, as well.

I pray for those who are not actively reading the Bible. Perhaps there are other things in their lives that take their time and energy, or they have been so wounded that they have turned their backs on you. Or maybe they have just made other things a priority. I pray that you would draw them back to yourself, dear Jesus.

I pray all this in your precious name, amen.

"All Scripture is inspired by God and is useful to teach us what is true and to make us realize what is wrong in our lives. It corrects us when we are wrong and teaches us to

do what is right. God uses it to prepare and equip his people to do every good work" (2 Tim. 3:16–17).

Journal Your Thoughts

Day 29

Prayer Against Double-Mindedness

Dear Abba, Father,

Depending on what is happening at any given moment, my attitude can change like the wind. I pray that I would not rely on my circumstances to dictate my choices. I want you, not the world, to drive my every decision.

I pray for those who continually struggle with double-mindedness. I am thinking of the ones who have so much to offer, but their decision-making flip-flops depending on their circumstances. I pray that they would draw closer to you so that you can strengthen them from the inside out. No more do they need to be slaves to the things happening around them, but a free person in Christ.

That is exciting to know that I can choose to be consistent in my choices. The world does not decide whether my choices are consistent or not—I do. If I relied on the wisdom of the world, I would fail most of the time. If I choose to be full of the joy and wisdom of Christ, I will live an abundant life. Your power, Lord, will surge through me and I will not fear, but trust in you. Thank you!

In Jesus' name I pray, amen.

"Do not waver, for a person with divided loyalty is as unsettled as a wave of the sea that is blown and tossed by the wind. Such people should not expect to receive anything from the Lord. Their loyalty is divided between God and the world, and they are unstable in everything they do" (James 1:6–8).

Journal Your Thoughts

Day 30

Prayer Against Being Judgmental

Dear Father God,

How easy it is to judge others, especially when I have a "log" in my own eye, as Jesus said. I fear how others judge me, as well. Instead of trusting what your Word says about me, I trust the opinion of others. Whether I am letting myself be judged or whether I am doing the judging, that cycle has to end.

The only one who has the right to judge another is the one who created them. That is true for others, and it is true for me. Only you have the right to judge me. You, dear Lord, made me perfect in your sight. I know that I have flaws that come from being human, but you are working those out for the good of the kingdom. I need only to be patient and trust.

I pray for _____ whom I have judged harshly. I repent and ask for your forgiveness, Lord. Please give me the strength and guidance to ask for their forgiveness. Help me to see them through your eyes, God. I pray for reconciliation in our relationship. We both said hurtful words, and I wish I could take mine back. Since I can't, I am grateful that I can pursue the process of reconciliation. Help me to be humble as I seek out _____. I pray that their heart and mind would be open to working things out with me.

I pray all this in your precious and holy name, amen.

"Do not judge others, and you will not be judged. For you will be treated as you treat others. The standard you use in judging is the standard by which you will be judged. And why worry about a speck in your friend's eye when you have a log in your own? How can you think of saying to your friend, 'Let me help you get rid of that speck in your eye,' when you can't see past the log in your own eye?

Hypocrite! First get rid of the log in your own eye; then you will see well enough to deal with the speck in your friend's eye" (Matt. 7:1-5).

Journal Your Thoughts

Day 31

Prayer Against Bitterness

Dear Heavenly Father,

Bitterness has deep roots. Once bitterness starts growing, it is very difficult to stop, for its roots spread far and wide. As the roots of my bitterness spread, the hurt that it causes doesn't affect only me. It affects every person I come in contact with. I know that is not what you have planned for me.

Lord, you know that letting go is not easy. Give me the strength to release that bitterness to you. Letting go of bitterness is so important that, when I hold something against someone, you don't want me bringing you my gifts until it is resolved. Before bringing any offering to you, you want me to try to reconcile with the one whom I have offended or who has offended me. It doesn't matter who started it. Jesus paid the price for it. This doesn't mean that Jesus doesn't care. He cares deeply, and he hurts with me in my pain.

Lord, I pray for _____, the one with whom I need to be reconciled. Jesus, in your name, I pray that their heart and mind would be open to what I have to say when I see them. I pray for their healing, as well as my own.

In Jesus' name I pray, amen.

"Look after each other so that none of you fails to receive the grace of God. Watch out that no poisonous root of bitterness grows up to trouble you, corrupting many"
(Heb. 12:15).

Journal Your Thoughts

Day 32

Prayer Against Having a Critical Spirit

Dear Lord,

Complain, complain, complain . . . that seems to be the norm for me sometimes. Nothing but complaints! Teach me to watch my words before they spill out of my mouth and cause destruction to others. May I not believe the lie that complaining makes me feel better.

You are doing so many good things in my life. When my day doesn't go the way I want it to, it is so easy to focus on the negative. Help me to focus on the positive instead. Transform my perspective. Help me to see what you see. Help me to see others through your eyes. If there is something that needs to be corrected, may it be filtered through a spirit of love and grace before I speak. If I need to correct someone, may I do it in a way that glorifies you.

I pray against having a critical spirit. I know how I feel when people complain to me about others, or complain about something I have said or done. It is discouraging. I want to be encouraging to others so that they will be filled with joy in all that they do. Let us encourage one another as long as we have breath to do it. I love how Jesus always encouraged, and he did it with great love. Let me follow his example.

In Jesus' name I pray, amen.

"May the words of my mouth and the meditation of my heart be pleasing to you, O Lord, my rock and my redeemer" (Psalm 19:14).

Journal Your Thoughts

Day 33

Prayer for Abiding in Christ

Dear Jesus,

I pray for all of us as we practice abiding in you. The practice of abiding needs to become a part of us so that it just comes naturally. "Naturally" means that we don't even have to think about it—we just do it. Only then can we fully gain all the blessings from your hand.

As we allow you to wash over us, you offer us the gifts of peace, rest, strength, trust, and so much more. May we steep in your presence, especially during the quiet times. You promise that you will always be with us, and I pray that we would consciously always be with you, too.

I pray specifically for those who are struggling. If they are not abiding in you, Christ Jesus, I pray that their hearts would be squeezed so that they become intent on seeking and spending more time with you. Your promise for them is the same as for me. You love us more than we can comprehend, and you desire us to spend time in your presence and stay connected to you, the Vine.

This day, I would like to take steps to walk closer with you, Jesus. The nearer I am to you, the more blessed I feel. I pray that the blessings I experience would become blessings for another. Please show me, Lord, who I am to share you with to encourage them to be strong in you.

In Jesus' name I pray, amen.

"I am the true grapevine, and my Father is the gardener. He cuts off every branch of mine that doesn't produce fruit, and he prunes the branches that do bear fruit so they will produce even more. You have already been pruned and purified by the message I have given you. Remain in me, and I will remain in you. For a branch cannot

produce fruit if it is severed from the vine, and you cannot be fruitful unless you remain in me. Yes, I am the vine; you are the branches. Those who remain in me, and I in them, will produce much fruit. For apart from me you can do nothing" (John 15:1-5).

Journal Your Thoughts

Day 34

Prayer for a Thankful Heart

Dear Father God,

Being thankful doesn't come naturally for any of us. Thankfulness needs to be developed through the Spirit of God. We have a tendency to look at the negative rather than the positive. I pray, Lord, that our hearts would be changed by your Holy Spirit so that thankfulness flows through us continually. There is so much to be thankful for every moment of every day. I pray that we would recognize the blessing of Jesus and be thankful for him as we start our infinite list of things for which to be thankful.

I pray for anyone who has an ungrateful heart. Joy isn't being displayed in their lives, and they seem not to see the positive side of things. I pray for a spiritual transformation so that they would be able to see that you are in control and how you love to give good things to your children. Even when negative things happen, there is always a purpose, and you will use those things for good.

Lord, I want an attitude of thankfulness towards you all the time. I pray that I would take the steps to make that happen. I pray that whenever I feel negative, I would stop that thought and focus on your blessings instead. Help me to remember that being thankful is my choice and is not based on my circumstances.

In Jesus' name I pray, amen.

"For the Lord is good. His unfailing love continues forever, and his faithfulness continues to each generation"
(Psalm 100:5).

Journal Your Thoughts

Day 35

Prayer of Thankfulness for the Blood of Jesus

Dear Lord,

I thank you for the great sacrifice you have made for me. You didn't have to suffer and die, but you did … just to save me from an eternity in hell. Your love is more powerful than hell's gates, and I am so thankful for that.

I pray for those who do not know you as Lord and Savior, for they go through life with no hope. If they hope in the world, that will lead them to destruction. May you bring people, situations, and your Word to them so they would be able to experience Jesus and desire a relationship with him. They will be blessed by walking with you through life.

I lift up those who don't know you, Lord, and who are struggling with challenges that only you can help them resolve. I pray that your Holy Spirit would take hold of them and show them the way to go. Jesus, you are the way, the truth, and the life, and they need to know that deep inside. Use me to show your light. I am yours.

In Jesus' name I pray, amen.

"Jesus told him, 'I am the way, the truth, and the life. No one can come to the Father except through me'"
(John 14:6).

Journal Your Thoughts

Day 36

Prayer for General Finances

Dear Jesus,

I praise you for all of the good things you have given me. If I tried to count all of the blessings you have provided, my list would never end. The blessings start as soon as I open my eyes each morning. Each new day is a precious gift. Thank you for your perfect provision, including food, shelter, relationships, and so much more.

You have instructed me how to use my finances wisely not only for myself but also for others. You bless me so that I can pass that blessing on to those around me. Thank you that there is no end to your resources. Your arm is never too short. I never need to fear that you will not provide for me. I only need to look at the flowers at my feet and the birds in the sky to see your faithfulness.

Nothing on this Earth belongs to me. In your grace, you have given me the privilege of being an overseer of the things you have chosen to give me. I pray that I would be wise in using the resources with which you've blessed me. I pray that I would refrain from buying things outside of your will. Instead, help me to be a good steward, choosing wisely the things that I need and not just that I want. I pray that greed, lust, despair, and other temptations would not sway me from using my finances to your glory.

In your name, amen.

"The master was full of praise. 'Well done, my good and faithful servant. You have been faithful in handling this small amount, so now I will give you many more responsibilities. Let's celebrate together'" (Matt. 25:21).

Journal Your Thoughts

Day 37

Prayer for Those Who Are Struggling to Make Ends Meet

Dear Father,

Thank you for all the blessings you give to me. Even though sometimes I struggle to make ends meet, you provide me with everything I truly need. I pray for those times when I trust the world more than I trust you. When I do not honor you in the care of my finances, there are consequences. I ask for healing from this.

So many people struggle with their decision-making as it relates to money. I pray that they would be empowered to learn how to manage it. I pray that sacrifice would become the norm more than the desire to have things *right now*. The world shouts out the message that we deserve everything. That is not your message, Lord. I pray that your truth would be louder than the message of the world.

Father, I pray for those who are having a hard time making ends meet. Show them the way, dear Lord, to financial freedom. I pray that they would come upon something or someone to help them learn how to manage their resources. You are the source of all things, and I thank you for your giving heart toward your children.

In Jesus' name I pray, amen.

"This same God who takes care of me will supply all your needs from his glorious riches, which have been given to us in Christ Jesus" (Phil. 4:19).

Journal Your Thoughts

_____
_____
_____
_____
_____
_____
_____
_____
_____
_____
_____
_____
_____
_____
_____
_____
_____
_____
_____
_____
_____
_____
_____
_____
_____

Day 38

Prayer for the United States

Dear Lord,

This country was built largely upon your precepts. In many ways, it has wandered so far. I pray that change would come. I pray that this change would start in individual hearts, beginning with mine. Touch my heart and change it. Help me to follow you alone and not the temptations of this world. I desire to be a tool used for your glory in encouraging others to follow you.

Lord, I pray that our nation would humble itself before you and repent. For many years, it has been a pinnacle of power and hope for many in the world, but there are areas in which we have forsaken your way. Much of our country has chosen to dwell in darkness and enjoy the pleasures of a season rather than experiencing your richness for eternity. Please forgive my part in this sinfulness.

I pray for healing for the nation that can come only from your hand, God. Like the paralytic who knew that he needed the healing touch of Jesus, this country needs to know that it needs your healing, too. I pray that a desire would grow across this land for healing from sin. Start with me, Lord. May seeking and obeying you be a choice I make daily. That is the only way I will know you more, and I want to better know and follow you.

In Jesus' name I pray, amen.

"Then if my people who are called by my name will humble themselves and pray and seek my face and turn from their wicked ways, I will hear from heaven and will forgive their sins and restore their land" (2 Chron. 7:14).

Journal Your Thoughts

Day 39

Prayer for the Church

Dear Heavenly Father,

The body of believers that you have created is the Church. It is not a building, but the people who are saved by your grace and who call themselves by your name. I pray for Christians to realize their important role in glorifying Jesus and expanding his kingdom. The Church is to be active and not passive in meeting this challenge.

Satan tries to create division inside the Church, and I confess that sometimes I give him a foothold. I pray that I and other Christians would be aware of his tactics and be proactive in preventing his schemes from taking hold inside the Body. I pray that every heart in the Church would join in this battle for unity through prayer. Thank you that your love connects us and enables us to love one another and the world.

Prayer is the glue that holds the Church together in your name, Lord. I know that great things can happen when we obey your Word and pray. There is nothing that outweighs obedience to you, God. You want your Church to be successful, but for this to happen, we must "have an ear" to hear your voice.

I pray that the activities of the Church would not crowd out our relationship with you, dear Lord. That is where inner strength is built, enabling us to stand against the arrows of Satan. The evil one is powerless against prayer. Draw your saints together to intercede for the Church.

In Jesus' name I pray, amen.

"So if there is any encouragement in Christ, any comfort from love, any participation in the Spirit, any affection and sympathy, complete my joy by being of the same mind, having the same love, being in full accord and of one mind"
(Phil. 2:1–2).

Journal Your Thoughts

Day 40

Prayer for Pastors

Dear Heavenly Father,

My pastor has a huge job in my church. He cares for so many people in so many ways, and I know that I have taken him for granted. Right now, I lift up _____ to you and pray your peace, strength, joy, and protection upon him as he serves you.

Protect his mind and heart, Lord, as he ministers to your people, for I know that can be a very difficult task. Satan is always seeking to trip up our pastors, and many have fallen victim to his temptations. I pray that my pastor would continually wear your armor.

I also pray for his spouse and children, for they, too, feel the stress of his position. They might even carry the weight of others' expectations of them. I pray that your Spirit would give them the freedom to be who you have created them to be and not what others think they should be.

Lord, may I call on you to help my pastor and other pastors each day, for they need prayer. They go into spiritual battle every morning and battle through the night. I pray that they would not become victims of the evil one. I pray for them, and may I make prayer for them a priority in my life.

In Jesus' name I pray, amen.

"Dear brothers and sisters, honor those who are your leaders in the Lord's work. They work hard among you and give you spiritual guidance. Show them great respect and wholehearted love because of their work. And live peacefully with each other" (1 Thess. 5:12–13).

Journal Your Thoughts

Day 41

Prayer for the Pastor's Spouse

Dear Heavenly Father,

The call you have on a man or woman does not affect them alone, but their spouse as well. A pastor and his spouse are held to a higher standard, and eyes are always on them. Sometimes it can feel paralyzing. The expectations on a pastor's wife are great—and sometimes, they are unrealistic. Often, these expectations make a pastor's spouse and his whole family feel as if they cannot be themselves. Whom can they trust? They can trust you.

They can trust that you will not only care for them directly but also will bring trusting friends into their lives—real friends on whom they can depend. They can trust that you will bring friends who will love them and pray for them out of genuine care and concern and not out of desire simply to be in the inner circle.

The call on a pastor's spouse is as important as the one on the pastors themselves. I pray that each pastor's wife would remain open to what you are calling her to do. I pray for peace in discerning the call on her life and knowing all that you have trusted her to do. I pray for strength of character, as hard situations inevitably arise within a church. I pray that you will protect their hearts.

I pray for those who are struggling in their role as a pastor's spouse. Help them to be strong and discern your will. The needs of a church and its people can seem overwhelming. Sometimes the boundaries of what to do and what not to do can be unclear. Give them wisdom in which "battles" to fight and which tasks to take on. Bless the work they do for you.

In Jesus' name I pray, amen.

"Trust in the Lord with all your heart; do not depend on your own understanding. Seek his will in all you do, and he will show you which path to take" (Prov. 3:5–6).

Journal Your Thoughts

Day 42

Prayer for Prayer Warriors

Dear Lord,

You have called special people to fight through the power of prayer. Prayer is the most effective weapon we have and calling on your name brings power to those serving you. Even if those called to be prayer warriors don't always know specifically what to pray for, they know you are calling them to pray. No matter what time of day or night you call them, they obey. They understand spiritual warfare.

Prayer warriors take seriously the armor of God (Eph. 6:10–18) and fit themselves daily with its protection as they go about their day. I pray for your protection over your warriors. Keep Satan away from them. They love to pray your Word, for it holds power. I pray that they would allow your truth to seep into their minds and souls, and that it would always be on their lips when prompted by your Holy Spirit.

Lord, I pray that you would fill all your prayer warriors with your Holy Spirit so that they could see clearly the way you want them to pray. They love to be in your throne room and to pour their offering of prayers into the bowl. Thank you, Lord, that we can talk to you at any time and you are always here to listen.

In Jesus' name I pray, amen.

"Pray in the Spirit at all times and on every occasion. Stay alert and be persistent in your prayers for all believers everywhere" (Eph. 6:18).

Journal Your Thoughts

Day 43

Prayer for Mission Workers

Dear Father God,

The unknown can be the most frightening thing on a mission's trip. Especially when these trips take you to different lands with very different cultures and people who speak a different language. It can be unnerving and sometimes frightening. Sometimes the people are friendly, but sometimes they are not.

The goal of the mission worker is to share the Word of God and help people understand how much he loves them and that he made a way to save them. But just as here in the United States, many don't want to hear. Sometimes they can be hostile and even dangerous.

God has a plan in each place you send these missionaries, and I pray for their protection. I also pray for their encouragement and for open doors as they perform their work day after day. I pray they would have boldness and confidence to step out in uncomfortable situations and share what you put on their hearts. I pray that the seeds they plant would grow, blossom, and bear much fruit.

I lift up all the missionary workers. I pray for protection over them and their families. I pray that they would never fall short in what you call them to do. The love of the Lord is on their lips. I pray that this promise would be taken to heart. Could we each take some responsibility in doing mission work and show our brothers and sisters that we share their commitment to spreading the love of Jesus?

In your name I pray, amen.

"Jesus came and told his disciples, 'I have been given all authority in heaven and on earth. Therefore, go and make disciples of all the nations, baptizing them in the name of the Father and the Son and the Holy Spirit. Teach these

new disciples to obey all the commands I have given you. And be sure of this: I am with you always, even to the end of the age'" (Matt. 28:18–20).

Journal Your Thoughts

Day 44

Prayer for Those Who Want to Serve

Dear Jesus,

A servant's heart is a gift to those who use it to honor you. I pray that mine would always be willing to grasp opportunities to help others in your name. Even if I feel that I am not gifted in something, if you are calling me to do it, I will trust you to provide all that I need.

I pray for those who are unsure of their spiritual gifts, but they desire to serve you, Lord. I pray for clarity as they discern the areas you have already planned for them. I ask that you would send people to encourage them in identifying and using their gifts. Your plan is perfect. I pray that they would not miss it.

It is a huge blessing to be obedient and serve as you call us. You take care of the details, and your goal is always the kingdom. I can count on that. Let my heart be pure as I work toward your goals and not my own.

Thank you for the many who serve. Some are up front and some are behind the scenes. Regardless of where they serve, I pray that their joy would be made complete by their offering and that they would see how you use what is offered. It is all yours, Jesus, so you get all the credit. Amen.

"Even the Son of Man came not to be served but to serve others and to give his life as a ransom for many"
(Mark 10:45).

Journal Your Thoughts

Day 45:

Prayer for Outreach to Others

Dear Jesus,

In the busyness of each day, sometimes I do not notice the people you have placed around me. I confess that I don't always take the time to really see them and care about their struggles the way you do.

I confess that this is often because I am too focused on my own problems. I may ask how they are doing, but do I really care? When they answer, do I really listen? Do I take the time to hear with my spiritual ears, not just my physical ones, so that I can discern what is really behind their words? You hear their cries, and I ask that you would help me hear them, too. Help me not to ignore those who are hurting and forgive me for any hardness in my heart.

Please turn my heart of stone into a heart of flesh toward hurting people. Transform me into the person I was meant to be. People have the highest value to you, and I pray that I would see them as you do. I choose to do that and glorify you.

I pray that we, the Church, your body, would make a huge difference in the lives of others. May we represent you and fulfill your desire for us to help each other grow closer to you. So many are lost and need healing from the Savior's hand. Help me take action. Help me to be your hands and feet in this world and reach out in your name, Jesus.

I ask all these things in your name, amen.

"[F]or I was hungry, and you fed me. I was thirsty, and you gave me a drink. I was a stranger, and you invited me into your home. I was naked, and you gave me clothing. I was sick, and you cared for me. I was in prison, and you visited me." Then these righteous ones will reply, "Lord, when did we ever see you hungry and feed you? Or thirsty and give you something to drink? Or a stranger and show you hospitality? Or naked and give you clothing? When did we ever see you sick or in prison and visit you?" And the King will say, "I tell you the truth, when you did it to one of the least of these my brothers and sisters, you were doing it to me" (Matt. 25:35-40).

Journal Your Thoughts

Day 46

Prayer to Be Salt and Light

Dear Jesus,

Your parable about salt and light clearly calls me to show your flavor and shine your light into a world that is dark and tasteless. What good am I if I do not serve the kingdom of God in this manner? Your expansion plan for heaven is to be our utmost passion in living. Your kingdom is to be our priority before all other things.

I pray, Lord, that I would be salt at those times when bland living is experienced. You empower me to make life "tasty" by showing your love, grace, and mercy. Each day, I have the opportunity to do this. I pray that I would actively seek out these opportunities and not just sit back and wait. Help me to be intentional.

Lord, your heart must break at all the darkness in the world. Evil thriving in the darkness may seem powerful, but once it is pierced by light, its power disappears. I pray for the Church to become a beaming light of righteousness that scatters the darkness from our midst.

As the Church, we have power because we reside in you. You will turn the chaos into peace, and the glory will be yours.

I ask all these things in Jesus' name, amen.

"You are the salt of the earth, but if salt has lost its taste, how shall its saltiness be restored? It is no longer good for anything except to be thrown out and trampled under people's feet. You are the light of the world. A city set on a hill cannot be hidden. Nor do people light a lamp and put it under a basket, but on a stand, and it gives light to all in the house. In the same way, let your light

shine before others, so that they may see your good works and give glory to your Father who is in heaven"
(Matt. 5:13–16).

Journal Your Thoughts

Day 47:

Prayer to Encourage and Build Others Up

Dear Jesus,

I know that my words carry weight in others' lives. I can use the words that come out of my mouth to build someone up or tear them down. To be helpful and encouraging, my words must flow from your heart. This means my own heart needs to be firmly connected to you.

I pray that my intention would always be to build others up, for we are to encourage each other daily. We were not meant to journey this life alone, but to journey with others who surround us with love, acceptance, and encouragement. I need others, and they need me. May I take my role seriously.

I pray today for those who need your help and encouragement. Lord, I pray that you would work through me to encourage those around me and help them to see their great value. I pray that I would see people with the value that you do and love them with your heart. May I never again carelessly say a prayer as if I am checking an item off my "to do" list, but rather make prayer for others a priority as I present their needs to you.

In Jesus' name I pray, amen.

"Let us hold tightly without wavering to the hope we affirm, for God can be trusted to keep his promise. Let us think of ways to motivate one another to acts of love and good works. And let us not neglect our meeting together, as some people do, but encourage one another, especially

now that the day of his return is drawing near"
(Heb. 10:23-25).

Journal Your Thoughts

Day 48

Prayer for Those Craving Love

Dear Jesus,

The feeling of not being loved is one of the worst feelings in the world. I pray that I would always remember that you love me so much that you gave your Son to die for me. You will never leave me. Thank you for this unconditional love that is so different from the love offered by the world.

I pray that I would not strive for the love of those in the world. If I do, I will always feel dissatisfied, for fallen people cannot love like you. The world desires self-gratification and keeps real love at a distance. Your love is completely real, and you want to keep me close. I desire your nearness, Lord.

I pray for those who feel that they need the world's acceptance and approval to be loved. They try to be perfect in the world's eyes, but always fall short. The world tells them that they are not good enough. Your message is that they are perfectly made and that you love them just as they are. You will walk with them to help them grow and be everything they were meant to be.

I pray that those craving love would grow closer to you. If you choose, use me to help that happen, Lord. Your power and love will draw each of them close to you.

In Jesus' name I pray, amen.

"Can anything ever separate us from Christ's love? Does it mean he no longer loves us if we have trouble or calamity, or are persecuted, or hungry, or destitute, or in danger, or threatened with death? (As the Scriptures say, 'For your sake we are killed every day; we are being slaughtered like sheep.') No, despite all these things, overwhelming victory

is ours through Christ, who loved us. And I am convinced that nothing can ever separate us from God's love. Neither death nor life, neither angels nor demons, neither our fears for today nor our worries about tomorrow—not even the powers of hell can separate us from God's love. No power in the sky above or in the earth below—indeed, nothing in all creation will ever be able to separate us from the love of God that is revealed in Christ Jesus our Lord" (Rom. 8:35–39).

Journal Your Thoughts

_____

_____

_____

_____

_____

_____

_____

_____

_____

_____

_____

_____

_____

Day 49

Prayer for a Passion for Evangelism

Dear Jesus,

Telling the world who you are is a purpose I share with all believers. Let every Christian be sensitive to your Spirit's leading in this area. I pray for the words to speak to those who do not know you so that they may be drawn to your saving power.

I pray for courage to bring your message to those to whom you send me. I want others to see that I have spent time with you and want to know more about the relationship we have. I want them to discover the changes you have made in my life. There was a time I was lost and seeking after my own pleasures, and now I have been given more than I could have imagined by serving you.

Thank you for the people who told me about you. They are precious to me. I pray right now for people who do not know you. Send the right people, whether me or someone else, to share Jesus' passionate love with them. I pray that the Holy Spirit would enlighten them to this truth and make it real to them.

In Jesus' name I pray, amen.

"The seeds of good deeds become a tree of life; a wise person wins friends" (Prov. 11:30).

Journal Your Thoughts

Day 50

Prayer for Those in Need

Dear Jesus,

When I see people in need, help me to respond the way you want me to. Forgive me when I don't. Help me to see people as you do and care for them with your love.

Help me to remember how you saved me, a needy person, too. You didn't shun me, but enveloped me in your loving arms. You picked me up out of the mire and set me on solid ground. You blessed me so that I can bless others.

It is difficult for me at times to help others in need. I have fears that block the path to helping them. I sometimes feel that I don't have the right skills. I fear that they might use me, or perhaps harm may come to me. You say that I need to be wise, but if I stick close to you, I will have the wisdom and direction I need. Make very clear to me the actions you want me to take.

I pray for people who are struggling with reaching out. Lord, I ask for your blessings to meet their every need. Discouragement seems to rob them of our joy and peace. Let those in desperate need know that you are near, that you will provide for them, and that you will never leave them nor forsake them.

In Jesus' name I pray, amen.

"If someone has enough money to live well and sees a brother or sister in need but shows no compassion—how can God's love be in that person? Dear children, let's not merely say that we love each other; let us show the truth by our actions. Our actions will show that we belong to the truth, so we will be confident when we stand before God" (1 John 3:17–19).

Journal Your Thoughts

Day 51

Prayer for the
Burning Evangelist

Dear Jesus,

There are so many who do not know you. I used to be one of them, but you sent someone to tell me about you and your promises. Thank you. There is a purpose for which I have been saved. That reason is to reach out to others and show them who you are. Lord, I pray that I would be a good witness for you. There are words in my heart from you that burn to get out to a hurting world.

I pray also for the evangelist who is discouraged by the world. Perhaps they are shunned or ignored. Their seeds of encouragement seem to be falling on hard ground. But only you, Lord, know what each seed will accomplish, because it is by your Spirit that people's eyes are opened to spiritual things. I pray that the evangelist's heart and soul would be refreshed by the flow of your living water. Make him or her aware of your presence and fill them with love that allows them to be used by you.

I pray for those who fear evangelism. They fear worldly things such as what others will think of them, what will happen if they are rejected, or what more this will require of them. They fear for their safety as they go forth and speak your Word. Yet this same Word tells us to "fear not." I pray for courage, strength, and insight for all those who go and speak in your name. I pray that they would fear not!

"You must worship Christ as Lord of your life. And if someone asks about your hope as a believer, always be ready to explain it" (1 Pet. 3:15).

Journal Your Thoughts

Day 52

Prayer for the Unsaved

Dear Lord,

I know that your heart is hurting for those who have not come to you. The world rebels against your teachings, and people think they know the right way to live. They feed off the lure of earthly things and all of the world's temptations, thinking they are getting ahead when they are falling further behind.

Thank you, God, that you will not stop pursuing them. I believe that you will continue to call their names and touch their hearts. I pray that they would choose to follow Jesus Christ, your Son. You will not give up on them, just as you didn't give up on me.

In that belief, I lift up those who don't know you as their Lord and Savior. I pray for their spiritual eyes to be opened. I care for these people, but I know you care for them so much more. Your Holy Spirit encourages me to bathe them in prayer and lift up these concerns to you. I trust that you have their best interests at heart.

You love every person and freely offer them the gift of eternal life. Lord, may it be that these hearts answer your call and that they fall on their knees in repentance. May those who don't have a personal relationship with you make the decision to become part of your family.

In your holy name, amen.

"However, those the Father has given me will come to me, and I will never reject them. For I have come down from heaven to do the will of God who sent me, not to do my own will. And this is the will of God, that I should not lose even one of all those he has given me, but that I should raise them up at the last day. For it is my Father's will

that all who see his Son and believe in him should have
eternal life. I will raise them up at the last day"
(John 6:37-40).

Journal Your Thoughts

_____
_____
_____
_____
_____
_____
_____
_____
_____
_____
_____
_____
_____
_____
_____
_____
_____
_____

Day 53

Prayer for Believers Who Have Turned Away from God

Dear Mighty God,

How many times have I turned my back on you? Not intentionally, but preferring my way to yours? In doing so, I have walked away from you. It is important for me to stay close to you and in constant obedience so that I do not stray.

I pray for those who have been away from you for a long time. You have not given up on them. You constantly pursue them with your love. You send people to remind them of what you have done for them. You bring evidence of your faithfulness that cannot be missed or explained away. You go after them with a passion because of the great love you have for them. That love is more than we can imagine.

I pray that the people of this country would humble themselves and turn towards you and away from sin. This country was established on your Word and is now seeing the consequences of walking away from your truth and not allowing your Word to be spoken in our public schools and government institutions. I pray that we would all bow down and ask for forgiveness and seek your ways once again. If we do, you promise that you will heal us.

In your name I pray, amen.

"Then if my people who are called by my name will humble themselves and pray and seek my face and turn from their wicked ways, I will hear from heaven and will forgive their sins and restore their land" (2 Chron. 7:14).

Journal Your Thoughts

Day 54

Prayer for the Slave Owner

Dear Heavenly Father,

Even in today's modern world, there are still people who try to own others. They enslave people and give them no compassion, no dignity, and no voice. Slave owners are scarred people inside who have been hurt; therefore, they hurt others. In their hurt, they have allowed Satan to reign in their lives. Now their focus is on money and whatever the world can offer. They have no love for people, but only want to use them.

I pray that the slave owner would be healed from the inside out. Lord, you are the one who does miracles, and I pray they would see the evil of what they do. May they be disgusted by it. I pray that they would repent from hurting others, including preying on the vulnerable for the sex industry. If they are enslaving people for manual labor, I pray that they would set those laborers free. If those people choose to continue to work for them, I pray that the slave owners would give them a fair share for the work that they do. I pray for a miracle.

Satan has a hold on the hearts of these people, and I pray that they would break free. I pray that they would encounter the person of Jesus, and like the apostle Paul on the road to Damascus, be stopped in their tracks as you confront them in their sin. I pray that they would encounter you, the living God, and obey you fully. I pray they would be found from being very lost.

In Jesus' name I pray, amen.

"For you have been called to live in freedom, my brothers and sisters. But don't use your freedom to satisfy your sinful nature. Instead, use your freedom to serve one another in love. For the whole law can be summed up in

this one command: 'Love your neighbor as yourself'"
(Gal. 5:13–14).

Journal Your Thoughts

Day 55

Prayer for Slaves

Dear Lord,

Many of us think that slavery is no longer an issue in this world, but that is far from the truth. Right now, millions of people are still enslaved in the labor and sex industries. It is hard to grasp the horror they endure, and I pray for their freedom and healing.

Thank you, Lord, for shining light on this evil. Many are either coerced or kidnapped into a life of slavery, or perhaps their family has sold them for money. I pray for those families who have made the choice to sell their children.

Lord, your heart breaks for all of these victims, but especially for the victims of human sex trafficking. They need to be rescued, and if not rescued, then I pray for opportunities for them to escape. Lord, I know that you will help them. They need to trust you. Perhaps they have never trusted anyone in their entire lives, but I pray they would learn to trust *you*.

I pray for the voiceless who feel powerless in their circumstances. Keep shining the light on these evils so that your people can work to abolish all forms of slavery from the earth. Forgive us, Father, for allowing this evil to occur. I pray that the world would turn its back on the sex industry and that there would be no one to buy the services for which people are enslaved.

In Jesus' name I pray, amen.

"For the Lord is the Spirit, and wherever the Spirit of the Lord is, there is freedom" (2 Cor. 3:17).

Journal Your Thoughts

Day 56

Prayer for the Captive

Dear Merciful Father,

Around the world, there are many who are being held captive. In many cases, they are pastors, missionaries, and others working for your kingdom. These faithful servants have been thrown into prison simply for sharing your love in areas where the gospel cannot be shared freely. In some cases, they sit for years before being released. Sometimes they are tortured. Other times, they die in prison or are killed.

Thank you for these men and women who are willing to risk their lives for your sake—to bring others to a saving knowledge of Jesus. Give them courage as they wait for their rescue. Bring their plight to the awareness of those who have the power to win their freedom. Soften the hearts of the captors so that they would be willing to release them. If military strength is what is necessary to get them out, Lord, send as many soldiers as necessary to set your workers free.

I pray for their captors. I pray that their eyes would be opened and that they would no longer desire to cause such suffering and pain. These prisoners have broken no law. They are only sharing your Word. I pray, too, for the captives who are imprisoned for simply disagreeing with the political system or perhaps for no reason at all. In your great mercy, I pray that you would set them all free.

In Jesus' name I pray, amen.

"The Spirit of the Lord is upon me, for he has anointed me to bring Good News to the poor. He has sent me to proclaim that captives will be released, that the blind will see, that the oppressed will be set free" (Luke 4:18).

Journal Your Thoughts

Day 57

Prayer for Racists and Those Affected by Racism

Dear Abba, Father.

When you created people, you created each one to be unique. Every one of us is fearfully and wonderfully made. In your boundless creativity, you designed people to be of different genders, races, and ethnicities so that we might complement one another as part of your perfect plan.

Why do people hate or treat others differently because of their skin color, their accent, or the country they are from? Is it because they grew up in a home where racism was practiced? Is it what they see on television? Is it what is modeled in the community around them?

Whatever their reason, Lord, racism is not of you. In your eyes, each one of us is precious and of infinite value. If anyone believes that someone else is "less than" because of their skin color or country of origin, convict their hearts and bring them to their knees in repentance, Lord.

I lift up those whose lives have been affected by the deep scars of racism. What terrible wounds they carry because of something over which they had no control. Bring healing to their hearts. Shower them with your love and remind them that their accent or skin color was not an accident. You created them, and you love them. Even when they face insults and injustice, remind them that you understand because you faced hatred, too. You died at the hands of those who hate.

God, thank you that we will live in eternity in a place with no hate, no fear, and no suspicion. We will love one another in you, and live in harmony with one another as brothers and sisters as you intended us to do.

Even so come, Lord Jesus.

"There is no longer Jew or Gentile, slave or free, male and female. For you are all one in Christ Jesus" (Gal. 3:28).

Journal Your Thoughts

Day 58

Prayer for Working People

Dear Heavenly Father,

You have given me the great gift of having a job to provide for my daily needs. Thank you that I can glorify you with my occupation and that I can work with joy. I can do this even at a job I don't like because, ultimately, I'm working for you. This brings great joy to my heart.

I pray that those who are working today, whether at home or in a workplace, would find true joy in their roles. I pray they would realize that they are working for you, not for themselves or anyone else. Give them a greater sense of purpose in their vocation and teach them life lessons through their work experiences.

Lord, I pray for opportunities to share who you are through my words and actions as I go about my day. I pray that I would not get distracted with the busyness of my tasks and miss the opportunities you set before me. Help me to express joy rather than frustration and to be helpful rather than complaining. May I be thankful for my job rather than feeling that my employer owes me something. My attitude orchestrates my demeanor, so I pray that others would see you in me.

Use me, Lord, in my workplace. If I can be of service to lift up a downcast heart, give me a word of encouragement so that your Spirit can transform that person's mind to peace.

I pray this in Jesus' name, amen.

"Work willingly at whatever you do, as though you were working for the Lord rather than for people. Remember that the Lord will give you an inheritance as your reward, and that the Master you are serving is Christ"
(Col. 3:23–24).

Journal Your Thoughts

Day 59

Prayer for When
We Are Overwhelmed

Precious Heavenly Father,

There is so much to do throughout each day that I can't seem to keep up. I have so much on my plate. Because of this, I feel anxious and tend to be forgetful of so many things. I pray that you would help me to prioritize my schedule. Help me to focus on the things that really matter—the things that must be done rather than things I simply would like to do.

I pray for anyone who feels overwhelmed by their circumstances. Trying to keep up with kids, appointments, schedules, households, and other responsibilities. External pressures, such as the Internet, social media, and peers, can add even more stress. I pray that you give them peace, and remind them that you are in control of every detail of their lives. Help us to remember that it's not our job to fix everything and everyone. That's your job. Help us to not try to take that job away from you.

For everyone who feels overwhelmed, may they be reminded that you are there to help them along the way and turn to you when they need it. Encourage them to rely on your strength rather than trying to do it all in their own strength.

I pray these things in the precious name of Jesus, amen!

"I look up to the mountains—does my help come from there? My help comes from the Lord, who made heaven and earth" (Psalm 121:1-2).

Journal Your Thoughts

Day 60

Prayer for Using Time Wisely

Dear Abba, Father,

Why do I always feel as if there are not enough hours in the day? You have given us twenty-four hours to use wisely, and I confess that I don't always use them that way.

I desire to become more organized and better manage my time so that there is balance in my life. I ask for forgiveness for cutting you out of my schedule when life gets busy. Time seems to be the easiest thing to cut, but in reality, spending time with you is what I need to be doing the most.

What would my life look like if I intentionally gave you more time, spent more time with hurting people, and committed to teaching your truths as you call me? I say I don't have enough time, but the truth is, I do. I simply don't prioritize the things that are most important to you. This truth is painful, and I ask for a change of heart. I want your priorities to be my priorities.

Today, I pray that I would make a difference in my schedule that would honor you. I want to know you more, Jesus. I know that if I give more of myself to you, then the other things in my life will fall into place. When my priorities are right, you will make my day fruitful.

In Jesus' name I pray, amen.

"Live wisely among those who are not believers, and make the most of every opportunity" (Col. 4:5).

Journal Your Thoughts

Day 61

Prayer for the Trainer and the Trainee

Dear Jesus,

It can be difficult to train or be trained by another. It is a journey that needs a lot of wisdom and prayer. Not all are natural teachers, and the responsibility of training someone can bring out the best and worst in all of us.

For those who are called to be trainers, I pray for a caring spirit and great patience. Let them take the mantle of a mentor, teaching with the heart of a servant rather than the heart of a taskmaster. May their encouraging demeanor bring joy and excitement in learning rather than resentment or impatience. All students learn at different levels, so I pray the trainer would be open to teaching at the level and in the style with which their student learns. May trainers be clear in their teaching and show good characteristics of performing the jobs.

Lord, I pray for those who are being trained, as well, and pray blessings over the experience. May they be open and willing to learn, even if the trainer is not perfectly equipped for the job. I pray that they not become discouraged if their first try isn't perfect. I pray they would be encouraged by the ground they have covered and all they have learned.

In your name I pray, amen.

"So Jesus called them together and said, 'You know that the rulers in this world lord it over their people, and officials flaunt their authority over those under them. But among you it will be different. Whoever wants to be a leader among you must be your servant, and whoever wants to be first among you must be the slave of everyone else'" (Mark 10:42-44).

Journal Your Thoughts

Day 62

Prayer for Firemen

Dear Lord,

Thank you for the sacrifice of our first responders, including firemen. These brave men and women play a huge part in helping people in disasters. They risk their lives to do what needs to be done to save others. Whether that is going into a burning building, diving into the water, or racing through the streets, they choose to risk their lives for the good of others.

I ask for protection upon their lives as they go into what are often high-risk or life-threatening situations. I pray for peace and calm over their families who are at home. I pray that our firemen would have supernatural wisdom and discernment in times of crisis and be able to help the people they are there to rescue.

Firemen become family to one another because they all understand that their lives depend on one another. When one falls, the others mourn their loss. They travel for miles to be at their funerals to show their respect for what their brethren have done. This reminds me of how we should react to other Christians when they suffer.

In Jesus' name I pray, amen.

"We know what real love is because Jesus gave up his life for us. So we also ought to give up our lives for our brothers and sisters" (1 John 3:16).

Journal Your Thoughts

Day 63

Prayer for Police Officers

Dear Lord,

It's difficult to uphold the law when there are those who are committed to breaking it. Unfortunately, there are many without respect for the law and even fewer who are tasked with upholding it. I pray for the officers who risk their lives day in and day out. They promise to protect the people, and they do what needs to be done to fulfill this promise.

I can't imagine what it is like to be the spouse of a police officer. There is a sense of worry with every siren they hear. I pray peace and calm over them and their children. Police officers are a brotherhood and sisterhood throughout the country. They are family. These brave officers go into danger when called, not knowing what they will face or whether they will go home to their families that day. For those who have been killed, I pray for their family left behind.

So many tensions in our society make the jobs of our police officers that much more difficult. Even the best, most heroic officers often face suspicion and hostility from those they are trying to serve. If there are police officers who are not honest, who do not have the best interest of all people at heart, and who are fueling this mistrust, I pray that they would be removed from their positions.

I pray protection around our police officers as they serve. I pray that their heroic actions would be noticed and not forgotten. You have equipped them to serve, and you have their lives in your hand. I lift up all our police officers and pray that you would stay close to them. I pray that their courage and bravery would not override their discernment.

In Jesus' name I pray, amen.

"So be strong and courageous! Do not be afraid and do not panic before them. For the Lord your God will

personally go ahead of you. He will neither fail you nor abandon you" (Deut. 31:6).

Journal Your Thoughts

Day 64

Prayer for School Personnel

Dear Lord,

It's not easy to be a teacher or a staff member at a school today. Yet, we rely on these committed men and women to educate our children and prepare them to go out into the work world or further their educations. All the responsibility that teachers carry is inspiring, especially considering the number of children who are often in their classrooms. I pray for obedience of the children to the teacher. I pray that the students would understand what is being taught, and if they don't, that they would be brave and ask questions.

It's not just the teachers who need prayer. I lift up the secretaries of our schools, as well. Secretaries wear many hats. They are secretaries, confidants, communications operators, clothes collection organizers, and so much more. Their days fly by as they are expected to meet the needs of so many people, not just the children but also parents, staff, and volunteers. I pray for strength as they go through each very busy day. Protect them from chaos and keep them at peace.

I also lift up the principals and vice principals who carry the responsibility of all aspects of the school on their shoulders. The responsibility is heavy, yet they love their jobs and the children for which they are responsible. I pray for wisdom as they make decisions that impact the lives of children for years to come. I pray that they have time to talk with the children when needed. If the children make wrong choices, I pray the principal would have wisdom in addressing them.

Finally, I lift up all of those who work in our schools, whether they are teachers, secretaries, janitors, administrators, or the people who serve in the cafeteria. I pray protection over the entire school and pray against any evil that wants to enter the doors or playground.

In Jesus' name I pray, amen.

"You yourself must be an example to them by doing good works of every kind. Let everything you do reflect the integrity and seriousness of your teaching. Teach the truth so that your teaching can't be criticized. Then those who oppose us will be ashamed and have nothing bad to say about us" (Titus 2:7-8).

Journal Your Thoughts

Day 65

Prayer for General Health Problems

Dear Creator of All Things,

You know of the health problems that afflict your children. You have the power needed to heal anyone, but for bigger reasons than I can comprehend, you may choose not to do so right away. In the lives of some, you may choose not to bring healing at all, at least not during our lifetimes on earth.

I ask in Jesus' name that you would heal all who are suffering with health issues quickly if it is your will and glorifies you. You do, however, promise perfect healing in heaven. There, we will not have any pain or illness—just perfection.

For all those who struggle with health issues, I pray that they would see a glimpse of your presence and feel the peace you have for them. I ask that your joy would flow through them during the darkest of days. Help them, O Lord, to remember that you have not left them, but are with them and will never leave them or forsake them. May you hold them close. Whisper sweet, calming words into their spirits and bring them into your perfect plan for them.

I pray that, as I pray for those I love, I would not lose heart, even if I do not see healing this side of heaven. You know exactly what you are doing, Lord, and you have all the power to do it. I trust you.

In your precious name, amen.

"He gives power to the weak and strength to the powerless. Even youths will become weak and tired, and young men will fall in exhaustion. But those who trust in the Lord will find new strength. They will soar high on

wings like eagles. They will run and not grow weary. They will walk and not faint" (Isa. 40:29-31).

Journal Your Thoughts

Day 66

Prayer for Those with Cancer

Dear Heavenly Father,

The diagnosis of cancer is terrifying. Whether it is a trial faced by me or someone I love, I pray that you would give me strength not to fear. It says in your Word that you are with me, you will strengthen me, and you will help me. But most importantly, you remind me of who you are—you are God. If I can grasp that truth, I am able to experience true peace in any and every situation.

Dear Lord, I am thankful that you are there for all of those who have cancer or love those who do. I ask you to bring healing, but mostly I ask for your peace to surround them and comfort them. I pray that nothing in this world, not even cancer, would stop them from being everything you have planned for them to be.

I praise you, Lord, for each one of us is fearfully and wonderfully made. Every cell is especially designed by you for your purpose. You have the power to turn the diagnosis around and provide a clean bill of health. It's not too hard for you, Lord. Be glorified in my offering of praise to you. Every disease is in your hands, and the control is yours.

In Jesus' name, amen.

"You will keep in perfect peace all who trust in you, all whose thoughts are fixed on you! Trust in the Lord always, for the Lord God is the eternal Rock"
(Isa. 26:3-4).

Journal Your Thoughts

Day 67

Prayer for the Loss of a Limb

Dear Precious Lord,

I cannot imagine what it is like for someone who has lost a limb. Many have lost arms or legs due to war, accident, or disease. Life is never the same for them. Something that has been a part of them for so long, and perhaps even taken for granted, is now taken away. Along with the physical pain, there is an emotional hurt of the loss. There can also be a loss of independence. Even a loss of identity.

I pray against any depression that tries to set in their minds. They are not to feel "less than" because of this loss. They are just as whole in you as they were before. You will continue to use them. Their story has not been completed, but some very interesting chapters are yet to come and that will give you glory, Lord.

I pray for those who have a disability from the loss of a limb. I pray blessings over their lives. Help them to see all the possibilities that are still before them. Help them not to fall into a victim mindset. This would be so detrimental to their progress. I pray they will soar.

In Jesus' name I pray, amen.

"It is the same way with the resurrection of the dead. Our earthly bodies are planted in the ground when we die, but they will be raised to live forever. Our bodies are buried in brokenness, but they will be raised in glory. They are buried in weakness, but they will be raised in strength" (1 Cor. 15:42–43).

Journal Your Thoughts

Day 68

Prayer for Those Suffering with Lingering Pain

Dear Jesus,

There are people who live with terrible pain day in and out, and I cannot imagine how they endure. Pain drains a person of their energy, patience, and outlook on life. Pain seems to numb them of the goodness around them, and sometimes it is all they can see. I pray for a new set of eyes for them—your eyes.

I pray for complete healing and that they live in obedience to you. Pain can make a person apathetic and unmotivated. I pray against those feelings, for they make it very difficult for people to serve you.

Much research has been done on how to control pain. I pray that a system is developed to help your children as they suffer daily. The steps they take to control the pain will enable them to go from feelings of victimization to victory. Empower them to choose between treatments that may or may not help.

How frustrating it must be! Lord, I pray for their commitment to keep seeking you in their treatment. You are the greatest Healer of all. I pray for you to touch them so they will be healed, and then share the power of your healing with others. You know the plan. You care for them and will help them in their time of need.

In Jesus' name, amen.

"Let all that I am praise the Lord; may I never forget the good things he does for me. He forgives all my sins and heals all my diseases" (Psalm 103:2–3).

Journal Your Thoughts

Day 69

Prayer for Those with Problems in Their Feet

Dear Father,

My feet are a wonderful gift you have given me. They help me get from one place to another. The feet are the hard workers of the body. They walk, run, dance, and move. They are expected to keep us up and moving to do good works. If I have a sore foot, it affects the entire direction of my day. I can be hindered by the pain. I can become impatient or irritable with others. I pray that your healing would come upon my feet and bring them to wholeness.

I pray for those who are bothered by their feet, whether it is due to hard, daily work; poor choices; or illness. Help them to take care of their feet the best they can, for they are a wise investment. Whether it's a foot bath, a massage, or just putting lotion on them after a hard day, help us all take better care of the feet that take such good care of us.

I pray for those who need healing over broken bones in the foot, torn ligaments, or any damage to their feet. Ingrown toenails can be painful. Over all these, I pray for healing. I pray that their feet will once again carry them to where you have them go in your name, amen.

"Don't you realize that your body is the temple of the Holy Spirit, who lives in you and was given to you by God? You do not belong to yourself, for God bought you with a high price. So you must honor God with your body"
(1 Cor. 6:19–20).

Journal Your Thoughts

Day 70

Prayer for Those with Sleep Disorders

Dear Jesus,

Sleep is a precious gift. Without proper sleep, everything is affected—our minds, our health, and our work for your kingdom. I pray for those who suffer from sleep apnea and other sleep disorders. I pray that their breathing be made smooth naturally or by the use of technology.

The first step is detection, so I pray that those who are not sleeping well would be willing to get the proper testing. The results could be lifesaving. I pray for the healing they need to get a good night's sleep. Driving can also be hazardous. If they fall asleep at the wheel, it's not only their lives at risk, but also those around them. Lord, I pray against these distractions.

I pray for those whose sleep is disrupted. Whether it's from a medical issue, a stressful life situation, or they are just burned out from the day. Lack of sleep affects everything in their life, and I pray for protection over them. They work hard, and when it is time for bed, they feel tired, but as the night goes on, their sleep is disrupted. I pray, Lord, that you give them a refreshing night of sleep that will help them regain their focus on all of their responsibilities during the day.

I lift up those who are sleeping too much. Sleep seems to run their lives. Oversleeping could be from a medical issue, or it could be due to depression or trying to escape overwhelming life situations. Whatever is at the root, I pray for you to step in and bring healing.

Thank you, Lord, for the gift of sleep. I appreciate the way we can be rejuvenated from some good sleep. In Jesus' name I pray, amen.

"You can go to bed without fear; you will lie down and sleep soundly" (Prov. 3:24).

Journal Your Thoughts

Day 71

Prayer for Those with a Terminal Illness

Dear Father God,

The news has been given to them from a doctor—terminal. How terrifying that must be! Whether they are given years to live or just days, weeks, or months, they have little hope of surviving. Where do they turn? In an instant, their life changes. Lord, I pray for them as they travel this journey. They do not walk alone. You have provided friends and family to help them. More importantly, you are with them.

I pray for all as they travel this journey of living with a terminal illness. I pray for a miracle of healing. If that is not your plan, Lord, then I pray that you bless them abundantly with your presence. It is amazing what you can do for someone when hope is ripped away from them. With you, there is always hope.

Bring people around them to love them, support them, and provide for their needs and also the needs of their families. Lift the burden upon these families, Lord. Put on the hearts of those around them to offer their time and their resources freely, whether it is helping with drives to the doctor, bringing a meal, or regular prayer.

Thank you for being there for those with terminal illness. I cannot imagine walking this road without you beside me. I pray encouragement for anyone who does not know you. I pray that a word of your hope be spoken to them and that they may see you for who you are, dear Lord. May they understand their need for you and begin this new season together with you.

In Jesus' name I pray, amen.

"I will never fail you. I will never abandon you"
(Heb. 13:5).

Journal Your Thoughts

Day 72

Prayer for the Homebound

Dear Precious Lord,

It is so hard to be at home all the time because of physical restraints. You have created such a beautiful world that it is heartbreaking not to be able to enjoy it as desired. I pray for grace for the one who needs to stay at home. May they be comforted by the friends and family who surround them. If it is your will, Lord, I pray that with help, they would be able to go outside their homes.

When the hours are long through the day, I pray for peace in your Spirit. Let your presence be known to them and that you are active and living in them. While they may feel alone, you will never leave them alone. I pray that other activities will be discovered that they can do, especially for you. How fulfilling that would be for them.

I pray for those who are struggling in this area. May their hearts be encouraged each day, knowing that you love them deeply. They have great worth and a purpose. Their story has not ended, but continues to be written. I pray that they see what it is you have for them to do. I pray for strength and encouragement to be found through your Word.

I pray this in your precious name, amen.

"For this world is not our permanent home; we are looking forward to a home yet to come" (Heb. 13:14).

Journal Your Thoughts

Day 73

Prayer for Those Who Suffer from Hoarding

Dear Father,

You are a God of abundance. We have no need to hoard, since you are all the abundance we need. Too many people miss that truth and fail to fully trust in you. But hoarding can also be an emotional disorder, and I pray that the one who suffers from hoarding will get help and healing.

Hoarding truly can be dangerous. I think of elderly people who can't get around their house because of all the items in the way or those who live in unhealthy and unsanitary conditions. Lord, I ask that those who suffer from hoarding be released from that prison and be free from the feel that they need to cling to material things. I pray they can throw away the clutter in their lives and allow you to move in.

Do I hoard, too, Lord? Do I hold on to any material thing that keeps you away from me? I pray for healing from that item that it may have no power over me. I pray that I would be able to show love and acceptance to others who are hoarding.

There is so much fear with hoarding. Anxiety is packed in along with the boxes that surround them. Your truth is the key to freedom, and I pray your power to show through.

In Jesus' name I pray, amen.

"Don't store up treasures here on earth, where moths eat them and rust destroys them, and where thieves break in and steal. Store your treasures in heaven, where moths and rust cannot destroy, and thieves do not break in and

steal. Wherever your treasure is, there the desires of your heart will also be" (Matt. 6:19–21).

Journal Your Thoughts

Day 74

Prayer for Those with Mental Illness

Dear Heavenly Father,

I pray for anyone who suffers from any type of mental illness. I know it can greatly affect the way they live. But I thank you that you have made a way for them to address these challenges, whether through a physician or natural remedies. I thank you that you are the great Healer. I pray healing over them and that, whether it is in their healing or the pursuit of their healing, they would glorify you.

If they need to seek help for their condition, I pray for guidance and direction. I pray peace for the sufferer as they discover, layer by layer, what is at the root of their struggles. If their illness is due to medical issues, I pray they would be open to the medication they need. If it is not due to medical issues, I pray that they would lean into you and find the source of their disorder.

Lord, you have created our minds with so much detail, and I thank you for that. When hurts from life affect us, they leave a scar, causing behavior that isn't the way you designed it to be, but that results from a disorder in the mind. You have gifted people to help with the healing process, and I pray that your power work through them as they meet with the ones who suffer any kind of mental disorder.

In Jesus' name I pray, amen.

"Don't be afraid, for I am with you. Don't be discouraged, for I am your God. I will strengthen you and help you. I will hold you up with my victorious right hand" (Isa. 41:10).

Journal Your Thoughts

Day 75

Prayer for Those Suffering from Depression

Dear Everlasting God,

Sadness drapes this world as the Prince of Darkness is always active in trying to destroy your people. I specifically pray for all who are suffering from depression. I pray that those who suffer would not give Satan a foothold in their lives, but would truly believe and apply your truth about who they are and whose they are.

Thank you that you have great plans for your children, and I pray that they would not believe the lies of the world. If they do, I pray that they would stop believing those lies and instead believe your truth.

I pray for your guidance and direction as I connect with those who are troubled and see only darkness ahead of them. I pray that my words would be anointed by you and give them light, encouragement, and hope.

Lord, if it is counseling that they need, I ask that you would supply good Christian counselors who would share your truth with them. I pray that your children would be healed by hearing your truth and that you would give their counselors or doctors wisdom in their time of need. If they need medication, I pray that they embrace it as a gift from you, and that they would rely on you more, because that is where the true healing will take place.

In Christ's name I pray, amen.

"I waited patiently for the Lord to help me, and he turned to me and heard my cry. He lifted me out of the pit of despair, out of the mud and the mire. He set my feet on solid ground and steadied me as I walked along. He has given me a new song to sing, a hymn of praise to our God.

Many will see what he has done and be amazed. They will
put their trust in the Lord" (Psalm 40:1-3).

Journal Your Thoughts

Day 76

Prayer for Those with Anxiety

Dear Lord,

Your Word tells me to not be anxious about anything, but to pray about everything and in all things give thanks to you. Through my prayers and petitions, I am claiming that you have complete control over the events in my life and in the lives of others. I do not need to fear what is ahead, for you are more than capable of handling every struggle.

I pray that when I start to feel anxious, I would turn to you for peace. Your presence will bring peace out of chaos. Your desire for me is to have peace. Your love will make that happen, but I need to believe you and stand on your Word. Help me to remember that peace is gained by standing steadfastly on your promises. If I am distracted by the world, I may fall into confusion and lose your peace.

I pray that I would listen to your voice and not the noise of the world, and that I would read your Word daily because it is the spiritual food I need to be strengthened from the inside out. I pray for your healing where the scars on my soul have created anxiety. I want to be strong and confident in you, dear Lord.

In your precious and holy name, I pray, amen.

"Don't be afraid, for I am with you. Don't be discouraged, for I am your God. I will strengthen you and help you. I will hold you up with my victorious right hand" (Isa. 41:10).

Journal Your Thoughts

Day 77

Prayer for Those with Eating Disorders

Dear Precious Jesus,

You gave us food as a blessing for our lives, but Satan can turn food into a weapon to destroy us. I pray for those with eating disorders like anorexia nervosa, bulimia, and binge eating disorder. These are more than poor health habits. They are serious mental illnesses that can be fatal. Even when people are in recovery, they can battle unhealthy thoughts for the rest of their lives.

I pray that each person with an eating disorder would get help. If they are not able to ask for help for themselves, I pray that their family or friends would intervene. Even if someone is a healthy weight, they can be destroying their body on the inside in a way that puts their lives at risk.

Eating disorders destroy friendships, family relationships, and marriages. Their thoughts about food and their body image can be obsessive, stealing the joy and purpose from their lives. They think about nothing but food, whether eating it or starving themselves of it, every moment of the day. Satan's ultimate desire is to use the eating disorder to kill your children.

Dear Jesus, help your children see their need for help. Give them a desire to live. Bring them to a point where they are willing to ask for help, whether through counseling, an outpatient treatment program, or an in-patient program if that is necessary. Help them see themselves as valuable and worthy of help. Give them eyes to see themselves through your eyes— beautiful and perfect just the way they are.

I ask in Jesus' name, amen.

"Thank you for making me so wonderfully complex! Your workmanship is marvelous—how well I know it"
(Psalm 139:14).

Journal Your Thoughts

Day 78

Prayer for Overcoming Fear

Dear Lord,

You have not given me a spirit of fear, but of courage. Throughout your Word, you tell me that I should not fear. Thank you that I can trust the truth that you are sovereign over all things. I pray that fear would not have a foothold in me at all.

I pray for peace for the mother who fears for her children. I pray for peace for the father who fears he will not be able to support his family. I pray for peace for the spirits of all individuals who struggle with uncertainty.

I know that my heart has a tendency to grow anxious, so I ask for your peace to cover me. Whether I am thirty thousand feet above the earth or a mile beneath it, you are there, Lord. Whether I am walking in the spotlight or through the darkness, your grace and power are with me. Thank you that I am never out of your reach.

Lord, may my words bring peace to others today. I seek your wisdom for speaking into the storm in another's life. Each person is so precious to you, and you desire for each of us to live in freedom. Thank you that you are a God of love, not of fear, and that we can trust you completely.

In Jesus' name I pray, amen.

"For God has not given us a spirit of fear and timidity, but of power, love, and self-discipline" (2 Tim. 1:7).

Journal Your Thoughts

Day 79

Prayer for Motivation

Dear Lord,

In this world there are many things that need to be done, and I sometimes feel unmotivated regarding the things you have called me to do. I pray against my feelings of lethargy. Help me choose to stay focused on what you want me to accomplish today. I do not want to give in to apathy.

I ask for your help and direction to complete the work you have given me and to do it full of fervor. May I not grow bored, but be refreshed and energized by your Holy Spirit to continue the race.

Show me, Lord, what is making me shrink from the tasks to which you are calling me. Am I fearful? Am I overwhelmed? I pray for clarity to know what is really holding me back. Reveal to me whatever it is that keeps me from fulfilling your call. It is your bidding that I crave to fulfill, and I want to be a good servant.

As you reveal what is holding me back, there may be pain, but it is worth it to me. These are the moments I experience your presence in a special way. My desire is to experience your presence in every area of my life, for I love you so much.

May my life bring glory to you.

In Jesus' name I pray, amen.

"Whatever you do, do well. For when you go to the grave, there will be no work or planning or knowledge or wisdom"
(Eccl. 9:10).

Journal Your Thoughts

Day 80

Prayer for Those with Mental Distress

Dear Heavenly Father,

I pray for anyone who suffers from any type of mental distress. I know it can greatly affect the way they live. Thank you that you have made a way for them to address these challenges, whether through a physician or natural remedies. Thank you that you are the great Healer. I pray healing over them and pray that they would use this as a way of glorifying you.

If they need to seek help for their condition, I pray for guidance and direction. I pray peace for the sufferer as they discover, layer by layer, what is at the root of their struggles. I pray that they would not lean into the medication, although at times it is needed. Better yet is to lean into you and find the source of their unrest.

Lord, you have created our minds with so much detail, and I thank you for that. When hurts from life affect us, they leave a scar, causing behavior that isn't the way you designed it to be. Sometimes it results from a disorder in the mind. You have gifted people to help with the healing process, and I pray for your power to work through them as they meet with the ones who suffer any kind of mental pain.

In Jesus' name I pray, amen.

"Don't be afraid, for I am with you. Don't be discouraged, for I am your God. I will strengthen you and help you. I will hold you up with my victorious right hand"
(Isa. 41:10).

Journal Your Thoughts

Day 81

Prayer for Priorities

Dear Lord,

My life is so busy right now, and there are many directions I can take. How do I know which direction to go? Your plan for me is perfect, and I want to follow it. I pray that I would not get sidetracked or focus on things that don't really matter.

During times of stillness and reflection, I am reminded of the good things that you have planned for me. It is essential that I take the time to seek you and look for your direction. The time and energy I invest in you is what really matters.

Our journey together, with my hand in yours, changes how I see the world. I can visualize you walking with me through times of ease and times of challenge. You point out what you would like me to see. Perhaps it is something beautiful that you have created. Perhaps it is something that breaks your heart, and your desire is for me to see it through your eyes and take action.

Investing in time with you is the most important thing I can do each day. You give more to me than I can imagine. Your love for me is overflowing. My cup can only be filled to the brim by you alone. No one or nothing else can do that. Thank you for satisfying me in your presence and leading me at all times.

In Jesus' name I pray, amen.

"Don't copy the behavior and customs of this world, but let God transform you into a new person by changing the way you think. Then you will learn to know God's will for you, which is good and pleasing and perfect" (Rom. 12:2).

Journal Your Thoughts

Day 82

Prayer Against Insecurity

Dear Father,

Each day, we do not know what will occur, and many of us have experienced tragic circumstances and events that make us feel insecure. Yet, your truth shows us that you are the greatest security we could ever have. You never slumber nor sleep, but are vigilant regarding all of your children, loving each one of us. You are always there. That is a secure feeling.

I pray for those who feel insecure. They have a lot of unanswered questions and are unsure which way to turn. They fear that they may lose everything. But the truth is, even if they lose every earthly thing, they will never lose you. You are more valuable than anything else. Plus, you promise to care for your children, no matter where they are or what they have done. Please draw them closer to you in this truth.

I pray for our country, which is feeling insecure amidst all of the frightening things happening in our nation and around the world. I pray for peace in the nation. I pray for national repentance so that the country would be healed. This healing will bring security like never experienced before. Lord, forgive us for our sin. I pray for restoration in our government. I pray for safety and security in every home. If you are at the center of a home, there will be peace.

In your name I pray, amen.

"Don't worry about anything; instead, pray about everything. Tell God what you need, and thank him for all he has done. Then you will experience God's peace, which exceeds anything we can understand. His peace will guard your hearts and minds as you live in Christ Jesus"
(Phil. 4:6-7).

Journal Your Thoughts

Day 83

Prayer for Those Who Are Lonely

Dear Jesus,

Life can seem like a long journey that we walk alone. Sometimes we simply feel alone. Other times, there are circumstances that do, in fact, leave us physically alone. Lord, you said, "It is not good for man to be alone." Even when we lose our loved ones, there are ways to become part of another community. I pray that those who are lonely will take the steps to join others.

Thank you that no matter how lonely we feel you surround us with opportunities to engage with others. You have made relationships for each of us to hold on to through both the good times and the storms. Thank you, Lord, for uplifting those who are brought low through loneliness. You want to encourage them with your love. In you, they are never truly alone. You are with them always.

God, I pray for those who have felt lonely for a long time. Give me the words to encourage them and remind them that even though they feel lonely, they are never alone. Help them to see the opportunities to build friendships and surround themselves with people who love them. Give them eyes to see the people you have sent, are sending, and will send in the future. I pray for boldness to step into those opportunities.

Please, may they never give up on developing relationships. Even if they are surrounded by others, may they still desire quiet time with you. Let them never forget that you are the truest friend and that knowing you is where the real growth happens.

In Jesus' name I pray, amen.

"There are 'friends' who destroy each other, but a real friend sticks closer than a brother" (Prov. 18:24).

Journal Your Thoughts

Day 84

Prayer for Those Who Want to Have Better Physical Fitness

Dear Lord,

It can be so hard for some to be fit with the body that you have given them. You want us to take care of our bodies, but sometimes wrong choices in activity, food, and other things cause our bodies to falter. I pray for those who need to be inspired to work at taking better care of their bodies. Good health is so important. Our bodies are the temple of the Holy Spirit.

I pray for those who desire to bring their bodies to a healthy weight. Even if they lack the desire to do so, I pray that you would motivate and energize them. Give them the energy they need to exercise. Give them the strength to resist the foods that are not good for them. In each step of the process, may they be encouraged by you and your Word. I pray that they would keep at it and not give up. Give them courage, dear Lord, to sacrifice unhealthy food and replace it with healthy food. Simple choices every day can make such a big difference.

For those with physical ailments that prevent them from exercising, I pray grace over them. I pray that they would find a way to do the best they can with what you have given them. I pray that health professionals would join them in discovering new ways of gaining fitness so that they, too, can live healthier lives. I pray that they would make better choices where needed, and if there is a sense of laziness, that you would take it away. Help them, Lord, to fight for fitness.

Amen.

"Don't you realize that your body is the temple of the Holy Spirit, who lives in you and was given to you by God? You do not belong to yourself, for God bought you with a high

price. So you must honor God with your body"
(1 Cor. 6:19-20).

Journal Your Thoughts

Day 85

Prayer for Those Experiencing Challenges

Dear Abba, Father,

Challenges come in many shapes and sizes. What matters is how we respond to them. I pray for grace for anyone going through a challenge right now. May they know they are not alone. If someone isn't being challenged now, they will be soon. God, you use challenges to shape and mold us into what you want us to be. Thank you for not leaving us as we are, but for using our struggles to help us become more than we could ever be when things are easy.

I pray for those having a hard time coping with their challenges. I pray that these challenges would not overtake them, for you are with them. May they stay focused and trust you, knowing that you will take care of the details. Help them learn and grow from the challenges they are facing, draw closer to you, and become stronger through them so that you can use them in a special way.

Thank you, Lord, for challenges. You allow us to struggle for a better purpose. For those facing challenges today, I pray protection over their hearts and minds as they walk through this season. I pray that their friends and family would step in to help them, encourage them, and point them in the right direction—towards you.

In Jesus' name I pray, amen.

"The Lord says, 'I will guide you along the best pathway for your life. I will advise you and watch over you'"
(Psalm 32:8).

Journal Your Thoughts

Day 86

Prayer for Those Who Are Indecisive

Dear Heavenly Father,

You have given me a mind for the purpose of using it. Your truth does not waver, and neither should my decisions. You offer me wisdom, and my responsibility is to ask for it and commit to being obedient to what I am shown.

Why are there still times that decisions seem so difficult to make? I want to do the right thing, but the world tells me that if I choose your way, I will offend people. I don't want to offend anyone, yet I know that pleasing you is more important. Doing what you want me to do gives you honor.

May I reject the "go with the flow" mindset in our culture and follow your decrees instead. My choices reflect who I am, which is a reflection of you. Whenever I feel indecisive, Lord, help me to remember to ask, "What would Jesus do?"

I pray for those who are having a hard time making important decisions. Give them wisdom and insight and help them stand firm on the choices they make. Send them people to pray for them, and with them, through whatever situation they are facing. I ask that the choice be clear to them.

In your precious name I pray, amen.

"If you need wisdom, ask our generous God, and he will give it to you. He will not rebuke you for asking" (James 1:5).

Journal Your Thoughts

Day 87

Prayer for Those Who Are Antisocial

Dear Lord,

What is it that makes a person antisocial? Whether it is personality or psychological disorder, I pray that they would be willing to come out of their shells. You designed us to be social beings and to work together with others. I pray for healing in the hearts of those who are antisocial as they interact with others each day and suffer in having to do so. Interactions are meant to be a blessing as we build each other up to do good works, but when a behavior walls a person in, it can be so difficult.

Lord, if there is any antisocial behavior in me, I pray that I would be healed from it. I want to be free of any bondage that prevents me from serving you fully. Perhaps I could help someone become stronger in social settings by being a safe person for them. I will not reject them, and I will accept them for who they are. Please help me help someone else.

Lord, I pray for those who want to be alone most of the time. I pray that you would help them to step out of their comfort zones and be involved with others. I pray for a spirit of encouragement for them to be able to interact with others on a daily basis and grow from these interactions.

In Jesus' name I pray, amen.

"So it is with Christ's body. We are many parts of one body, and we all belong to each other" (Rom. 12:5).

Journal Your Thoughts

Day 88

Prayer for Those
Who Want Control

Dear Lord,

The desire for control stems from a deeply seeded fear. When people think they are in control, they have the illusion of being safe. In reality, it is only when we can release control to you that safety truly comes.

I pray for areas in my life where I have a tendency to try to control. Not only does this desire not benefit me, but also it is a lie. I don't have the power to control my life. Only you have the power to do that. Give me the courage to release the steering wheel and leave the driving to you.

I pray for those who have controlling natures. I pray that they would see how their behavior affects others. I pray that they would become free from the need for control. They are meant to live in peace and freedom, and being free from the bondage of control will change their lives dramatically. By releasing control, they will gain freedom. In this freedom, there is joy.

Thank you, Lord, for being in control. I feel safe knowing that I only need to seek you and obey. You do not guarantee that the road will be smooth, but you do guarantee that I will be headed in the right direction. You will take care of me, no matter what occurs.

In your precious name I pray, amen.

"Look here, you who say, 'Today or tomorrow we are going to a certain town and will stay there a year. We will do business there and make a profit.' How do you know what your life will be like tomorrow? Your life is like the morning

fog—it's here a little while, then it's gone"
(James 4:13–14).

Journal Your Thoughts

_____
_____
_____
_____
_____
_____
_____
_____
_____
_____
_____
_____
_____
_____
_____
_____
_____
_____
_____
_____
_____

Day 89

Prayer to Be Better Organized

Dear Lord,

You are a God of order. You desire order for your children, as we are a reflection of you. I pray for the gift of organization. I know that I have trouble staying organized, but I know there is grace to get me through it. Thank you for the numerous sources available to help me, but the first step is to choose to use them. No excuses! Just get organized.

I pray for those who live as if they are always putting out a fire. They run from one thing to the next, trying to douse the flames. Every time they put out one fire, another seems to ignite. They spend their time running around putting out fires, and instead of moving forward, they end up back where they started. Help them get organized and be free from the chaos that disorganization can cause.

Lord, I pray for *shalom* in my life. I pray that all would be made smooth by your holy hand. It feels so much better when things are organized, so I pray that I would be abundantly aware and enabled when it's time to declutter the clutter. Give me the strength to do it and do it joyfully.

Thank you, Lord Jesus, amen.

"But be sure that everything is done properly and in order" (1 Cor. 14:40).

Journal Your Thoughts

Day 90

Prayer for Godly Marriages

Dear God,

You have established the covenant of marriage. It is a commitment made between a man and a woman to love and cherish each other throughout the rest of their days. This cannot be done without you. You are the creator of love, and you model what steadfast love is.

Marriage is hard, and couples cannot do this on their own. But when both depend on you, you equip them to be strong enough to endure all the struggles a marriage can bring. You walk with them and guide them through the journey.

Lord, I pray for those who are preparing for their marriages. The wedding day is coming and the celebration will be grand, but when everyday life begins, the couple will need your help daily.

I pray for the marriages that are struggling. Please heal them, Lord. Fill the hearts of these couples with forgiveness and renew their love for one another.

In Jesus' name I pray, amen.

"Love is patient and kind. Love is not jealous or boastful or proud or rude. It does not demand its own way. It is not irritable, and it keeps no record of being wronged. It does not rejoice about injustice but rejoices whenever the truth wins out. Love never gives up, never loses faith, is always hopeful, and endures through every circumstance. Prophecy and speaking in unknown languages and special knowledge will become useless. But love will last forever!"
(1 Cor. 13:4–8).

Journal Your Thoughts

Day 91

Prayer for Those Who Desire Godly Marriage but Are Single

Dear Lord,

I pray for those who do not have a spouse and desire to have one. It is not your will for everyone to be married, but when it is, I pray that they would be obedient in following your direction during this season of waiting.

I pray that they would not get impatient and rush into a wrong relationship. It's much more painful acting on impatience and suffering the consequences than being at peace while waiting patiently.

I ask you to show them ways to deal with their longing for marriage and ways to live a fulfilling and abundant life in you. You are the only one who truly offers a satisfying life. No human being can fulfill us the way you do. May you use this season of waiting to grow them, mature them, and allow them to become all that you want them to be so that they will be ready when you do bring them the spouse you have planned for them.

I pray that you would give them discernment, too, for there are wolves roaming about in sheep's clothing. Do not let them be deceived.

I lift up these requests and place them in your capable hands.

In Jesus' name I pray, amen.

"Take delight in the Lord, and he will give you your heart's desires" (Psalm 37:4).

Journal Your Thoughts

Day 92

Prayer for Children

Dear Lord,

Children are such a wonderful gift from you. Their young eyes, ears, and minds are hungry to learn. I pray that they would learn your truths about who they are and grow in confidence. May they experience your presence each day and grow up knowing that you are in charge and that you love them greatly.

I pray against any evil targeted at children. The destruction of wickedness is my desire. Surround every child with your vast army of angels and keep them safe.

I lift up the many children who don't have homes or families. These precious souls have so much to offer the world. I pray for them to be adopted into earthly families, just as we are adopted into your eternal family.

I pray that schools once again can become safe havens for children, where they can learn without fear. Thank you for the provision of school staff, teachers, and volunteers who give so much to them. I pray against any evil that tries to thwart the peace that should dwell in our schools.

I pray for godly parents to raise their children using your Word as a guide. Give them strength and discernment during times of challenge, for you will show them the way.

In your name I pray, amen.

"One day some parents brought their children to Jesus so he could touch and bless them. But the disciples scolded the parents for bothering him. When Jesus saw what was happening, he was angry with his disciples. He said to them, 'Let the children come to me. Don't stop them! For the Kingdom of God belongs to those who are like these

children. I tell you the truth, anyone who doesn't receive the Kingdom of God like a child will never enter it.' Then he took the children in his arms and placed his hands on their heads and blessed them" (Mark 10:13-16).

Journal Your Thoughts

Day 93

Prayer for Those Without Parents

Dear Father,

On this earth, children are often left parentless. Whether one or both parents are not present by choice, death, or other means, this leaves a terrible void. Children are left feeling unwanted, abandoned, and alone. You designed us, Lord, to be part of a loving family. That is the one place they should feel unconditionally loved, although we know that many children never experience this love.

I pray for children and adults who have lost one or both parents. They may feel abandoned and struggle with loneliness or rejection. This can be especially hard on special occasions when parents are expected to be present. I pray for someone to step into that role, whether that is a family member, a teacher, or someone from the community. The value these children will feel will last a long time.

Lord, may each of these lives thrive because of the love you give them and the love given by others whom you have called. May I, as one of the village of believers and followers of Jesus Christ, strongly impact the lives of children.

In your name I pray, amen.

"See how very much our Father loves us, for he calls us his children, and that is what we are! But the people who belong to this world don't recognize that we are God's children because they don't know him" (1 John 3:1).

Journal Your Thoughts

Day 94

Prayer for Relationships

Dear Jesus,

Your creation of mankind is amazing. You knit each person in their mother's womb to fulfill your will, and you know us all intimately.

Thank you, Lord, for creating me. You have placed people in my life, knowing that some are very different from me. This is enriching, but it also can be difficult. Thank you for the blessing of friends and family, and thank you for using difficult people to teach me how to love and accept others just as you love and accept me—just as they are. I want to be intentional and pursue relationships just as you pursue a relationship with me.

I confess that I am struggling in my relationship with _____. I pray for a desire for reconciliation. I realize that reconciliation may not occur, but let it not be because of me. I believe you want me to extend grace in the relationship. Peace is given and received through forgiveness. Thank you that I can experience your peace when I am obedient.

I've been hurt by relationships, and ask you to heal me. Our relationship with you is of the utmost importance. I believe that receiving your love, as well as pouring out my love back to you, will improve the other relationships in my life.

In your precious and holy name, I pray, amen.

"Don't repay evil for evil. Don't retaliate with insults when people insult you. Instead, pay them back with a blessing. That is what God has called you to do, and he will grant you his blessing" (1 Pet. 3:9).

Journal Your Thoughts

Day 95

Prayer for Reconciliation

Dear Lord,

Thank you for the relationships you have given to us. These relationships help mold and shape us into the people you want us to be. Sometimes there are conflicts that cause distance between people and disruption in their relationships. This is sad, but you know the larger purpose. Sometimes separation does need to happen, but sometimes there is a call for reconciliation.

Lord, I have two people on my heart right now that I pray will reconcile. _____ and _____ are distant from one another because of what seem to be irreconcilable differences, but Lord, you can always make a way. I pray that their hearts and eyes would be open to what you would have them do.

Lord, you are the Master Reconciler. You desire your people not only to reconcile between themselves, but also with you, and that's part of my call in evangelism. I am to speak your truth in love in order to point your children to you. I am the hands and feet of Jesus, and I am to go into the world to reach out to those who are separated from you. I pray that they would see your great love through me in all I say and do. Show me the way, Jesus.

I pray all this in your precious name, amen.

"All of this is a gift from God, who brought us back to himself through Christ. And God has given us this task of reconciling people to him. For God was in Christ, reconciling the world to himself, no longer counting people's sins against them. And he gave us this wonderful message of reconciliation. So we are Christ's

ambassadors; God is making his appeal through us. We speak for Christ when we plead, 'Come back to God!'"
(2 Cor. 5:18–20).

Journal Your Thoughts

_____

_____

_____

_____

_____

_____

_____

_____

_____

_____

_____

_____

_____

_____

_____

_____

_____

_____

_____

Day 96

Prayer for Adoption Challenges

Dear Precious Lord,

I pray that you would bless the families who are in the process of adopting. This process takes a lot of time, energy, and financial resources. Frustration can set in if things are not moving ahead as expected. There can be unexpected roadblocks and delays. For all who are currently in the process, I pray for encouragement and stamina as they fill out all of the forms, go through all the necessary checks, and work toward bringing home a new son or daughter.

I pray for comfort in disappointment, too. Many times, a couple will be given good news of the availability of a child, only for these hopes to be dashed. I pray that you would heal their hearts and encourage them to try again. Whether it was due to a last-minute decision by the mother, a country changing their laws on adoption, or other reason, it is painful.

Thank you, Father, that you have adopted us into your family, and this adoption can never be taken from us. Thank you for this model of unconditional love and patience for how we are to approach earthly adoption. So many children are in need of a forever family, and there are so many parents who desire to love them. Bring these children and parents together, Lord. Resolve any issues holding back the process of uniting children and their new homes.

In Jesus' name I pray, amen.

"God decided in advance to adopt us into his own family by bringing us to himself through Jesus Christ. This is what he wanted to do, and it gave him great pleasure"
(Eph. 1:5).

Journal Your Thoughts

Day 97

Prayer for Contentment in Singleness

Dear Lord,

I pray for those who are single. Whether it is a decision they have made, whether they are in a period of waiting, or whether singleness is something to which you have called them, there are times that they feel alone. That is a very difficult emotion to deal with. Even if they are not physically alone and they have friends and family to support them, they may still feel that way. We are designed for intimate human contact, and while you are there for them, it is still difficult.

God, I pray specifically for _____. If it is your call on their life that they be single, I ask you to give them contentment and remind them that their true security is in you, and none other. Give them courage when they are invited to a function that is attended mostly by couples, and give them a good spirit as they go. I also ask that if you do have a special person in mind for them, that you would give them patience and vision to recognize that person in your perfect timing.

I pray that they would have joy in this season of being single. Help them recognize the special way you bless them and enable them to do things for you that would be difficult if they were married.

In Jesus' name I pray, amen.

"So I say to those who aren't married and to widows—it's better to stay unmarried, just as I am. But if they can't control themselves, they should go ahead and marry. It's better to marry than to burn with lust" (1 Cor. 7:8-9).

Journal Your Thoughts

Day 98

Prayer for Difficult or Struggling Marriages

Dear Heavenly Father,

Marriage is hard at times. You know this, Lord, which is why you made yourself the third strand in the braid of marriage. You are the strong cord that will keep married couples together, no matter what comes their way. Whether it be problems of finances, fidelity, health, or other human need, you will guide them through their struggles and lead them to a place of peace and healing.

Lord, I specifically pray for marriages that are struggling. I pray for understanding, along with compassion, mercy, and forgiveness. Give these couples the strength to work through their issues and allow you to heal their wounds. You have great plans for them, and I pray that they would seek you during this time and find what they need in you.

The vows they spoke at their wedding were not merely words, but covenant promises. If either spouse decides not to fulfill their commitment, I ask that you convict their hearts and bring them back to where they need to be. Take them by the hand and show them the right path to be blessed.

In your name I pray, amen.

"A person standing alone can be attacked and defeated, but two can stand back-to-back and conquer. Three are even better, for a triple-braided cord is not easily broken"
(Eccl. 4:12).

Journal Your Thoughts

Day 99

Prayer for All Marriages

Dear Jesus,

Many couples run into tough times as they live their married lives together. I pray that they would stay close to you as the months, years, and decades roll by. There are so many joys for them to experience. I pray that they would rely on your promises and work together in love and respect as they walk through the journey together.

Your plan for them is good. I pray that they would seek that plan and follow it. You alone can heal hurts, and I pray for marriages that are experiencing great pain. Cover them with your peace, Lord, so that they forgive and take steps to better their relationship.

I especially think of situations in which the spouses feel they cannot salvage their marriage. It's tempting to think that there is too much hurt, too much damage, and too much broken trust to repair. I pray, Lord, that you would show them how you are the Great Reconciler and can work in them for healing and restoration.

I thank you, God, for marriage. The union between a man and a woman is made by you, and you say in the Bible that no man should tear it apart. Bind these husbands and wives close together, I pray, so that the enemy cannot get a foothold and that you would be glorified.

In your precious name I pray, amen.

"This explains why a man leaves his father and mother and is joined to his wife, and the two are united into one"
(Gen. 2:24).

Journal Your Thoughts

Day 100

Prayer for Struggling Families

Dear Abba, Father,

The family consists of people you have brought together in many ways, whether by marriage, birth, or choice to share life together. I wish all circumstances would go smoothly within the family unit.

Yet, this is not a perfect world, and there is sin, pain, and separation. If there is brokenness in the relationship, Lord, I pray for reconciliation, and that measures would be taken to build families stronger once again. So many things are tearing families apart. I pray that you would protect each member of the family as they work out their difficulties and stay together, living joyful lives.

I lift up the families that have experienced many difficulties and whose scars are beginning to show. Lord, bring peace into these families. Protect their hearts and minds, especially the children. I pray they would experience your presence as they journey through life's hills and valleys. Show them the way they should go, dear Lord. Encourage them with your Holy Spirit to live obediently to you, for then they will see your face and be healed. Then they can glorify your name through the testimony of your work in their lives.

In Jesus' name I pray, amen.

"Make allowance for each other's faults, and forgive anyone who offends you. Remember, the Lord forgave you, so you must forgive others" (Col. 3:13).

Journal Your Thoughts

Day 101

Prayer for Pet Owners

Dear Lord,

Everything you have created is beautiful, including our pets. Thank you for the many species that surround us. Pets bring us great company and put smiles on the faces of many.

Caring for a pet can be costly, and I pray for the pet owners whose finances are tight and who are unsure how they can afford to keep their pets. Or for those whose living situations don't allow them to keep them. Our love for our pets is deep and real, and many don't want to neglect them in any way. Sometimes, however, people must make a choice between pet care and other living or financial responsibilities. I pray, Lord, that you would give them discernment in those choices. I pray for those who own a pet and ask that you bless them as they care for them.

I pray for comfort for those who may have lost their pets either by loss or death. It is painful to have something you love so deeply ripped from your life. It changes you. I pray for peace as they seek a new normal after the loss of their friend.

I know that you care about pets because you care about all of creation. You even care for pets that are strays, and I pray that good homes would be found for them and that the owners would take good care of them.

In Jesus' name I pray, amen.

"The eyes of all look to you in hope; you give them their food as they need it. When you open your hand, you satisfy the hunger and thirst of every living thing. The Lord is righteous in everything he does; he is filled with kindness" (Psalm 145:15–17).

Journal Your Thoughts

Day 102

Prayer for Those
Wounded by Their Mothers

Dear Heavenly Father,

In your Word, mothers are described as being a great blessing. The Proverbs 31 woman is lifted up as a model, but we know that not every mother looks like this. Many mothers are deeply unhealthy, and in some families, dysfunctional cycles are being repeated.

Too many children are hurt by mothers who do not care for them properly, who abuse them, or who emotionally wound or ignore them. These scars are deep, and they can stay with the child forever, even as they grow into adulthood. Only through your healing they can become free from those hurts.

Lord, I pray for all those with wounds as a result of the hurtful behavior of their mothers. If their mothers are still alive, I pray, Lord, that they would be reconciled. I pray that these mothers would see their sin and repent from it. I pray that the child would offer mercy and grace to the mother so that healing can begin.

Forgiveness sets the prisoner free. There are no winners in bitterness, but all can win in forgiveness. If a child's mother is no longer alive, I pray that you would give the child the strength to extend that forgiveness, even when there is no chance of hearing "I'm sorry" on this side of the grave. I pray that they would release all of the hurt to you.

I pray for the other family members who have been affected by this hurt. May their hearts also be encouraged as you work in the lives of all involved. I pray they would not feel the need to choose sides and, instead, work to bring the separated together.

In Jesus' name I pray, amen.

"Hatred stirs up quarrels, but love makes up for all offenses" (Prov. 10:12).

Journal Your Thoughts

Day 103

Prayer for Those Wounded by Their Fathers

Dear Lord,

Fathers are seen as images of you. How devastating it can be when a father does not fulfill his role and damages the hearts of the family.

Lord, if there is a father who is controlled by ungodly behavior, such as drug or alcohol abuse, gambling, or ungodly sexual relationships, or who suffers from anger issues or other emotional sins, that they would be willing to repent. Squeeze their hearts, God, and give them the desire to make changes in their lives.

For the children who have received soul wounds from their fathers, I pray for healing. I pray that they would understand that while their earthly fathers may have failed them, you never will. Help them to understand that their earthly father does not represent you. Give them the boldness and confidence to come to you without fear. You welcome them with open arms, and I pray that they would sense your presence and seek you for healing. Make them strong, I pray, so that they can stand up under the weight of the sins of the father who hurt them and, ultimately, forgive.

I pray for those who have been repeatedly hurt by their fathers. Their souls have been scarred, and this damage has affected them deeply. If they are imprisoned by bitterness, set them free, dear Lord, and allow them to live lives of joy as they have never experienced.

In Jesus' name, amen.

"Fathers, do not aggravate your children, or they will become discouraged" (Col. 3:21).

Journal Your Thoughts

Day 104

Prayer for Those Wounded by a Brother

Dear Lord,

I pray for those who have been wounded by their brothers. It may have been a hurt caused by words, actions, or separation. Whatever the reason, the family has been scarred, and they are bleeding inside. I pray that healing would take place in each life that was affected. If trust has been broken, Lord, I pray for the offender and for the one offended so that they could each see their responsibility in the situation and forgive.

I pray for those who have been carrying heavy hearts for a long time in regard to their brothers. If family members have become estranged, I pray for wisdom and reconciliation. It is confusing to miss a family member, yet still not want to see them. I pray for restoration of the relationship.

Brothers have a great role in the family. They are looked up to and honored by the family; however, when sin enters the picture, their role can be warped. I pray for clarity as they become the brother they were meant to be. I pray that they would allow all worldliness to drop away and that they would pick up the cross of Christ.

In Jesus' name I pray, amen.

"So if you are presenting a sacrifice at the altar in the Temple and you suddenly remember that someone has something against you, leave your sacrifice there at the altar. Go and be reconciled to that person. Then come and offer your sacrifice to God" (Matt. 5:23–24).

Journal Your Thoughts

Day 105

Prayer for Those Wounded by a Sister

Dear Jesus,

Sisters have a special role in the family. They are friends and supporters of their siblings and the daughter of their parents. The sin of the world sometimes gets into a sister and they make wrong choices that affect not only themselves, but also others. Words and actions can wound deeply.

Where trust has been broken by a sister, I ask that she repents and turns anew to a relationship with you, dear Lord. I ask for reconciliation in the family.

I pray for anyone who has been hurt by a sister. I pray for comfort and encouragement as they find a way to come to terms with the situation. I pray that your Holy Spirit would lead and guide everyone involved and that each person involved would grow and heal through it. May they have a spirit of grace and mercy. Forgiveness is the key to freedom from bitterness. Squeeze their hearts to desire reconciliation. Send people to help them process the pain and learn about your wisdom in the matter. I pray for total and complete healing.

In Jesus' name I pray, amen.

"If another believer sins, rebuke that person; then if there is repentance, forgive. Even if that person wrongs you seven times a day and each time turns again and asks forgiveness, you must forgive" (Luke 17:3–4).

Journal Your Thoughts

Day 106

Prayer for Those Wounded by a Relative

Dear Abba, Father,

I pray that the wounds caused by a relative would be forgiven in your name and power. Whether the relative is alive or deceased, the injury can still seem so fresh. Hurts that have not been dealt with can take over a person's heart and mind, and I pray that they would be set free from them. It is to no one's benefit to keep the bitterness of the offense alive—not to the person who offended nor to the person who was wounded. Holding on to an offense only deepens the injury and wounds the injured person even more.

I pray for all those who have been hurt in some way by a relative. I ask that they would be healed from this devastating event. I pray that, if needed, they meet with a Christian counselor to work through the pain and find a new strength in you, dear Lord. I pray that they would see themselves as a wonderful creation made and loved by you. You will never leave them nor forsake them. This is your promise, and I pray that they would believe that to the fullest.

Father, I pray that all who have been hurt by relatives would not feel ashamed but become bold in their determination to heal. May they extend forgiveness to the offender. I pray that they would grasp on to you for direction in this journey of restoration and healing in their lives.

In Jesus' name I pray, amen.

"Don't be selfish; don't try to impress others. Be humble, thinking of others as better than yourselves. Don't look out only for your own interests, but take an interest in others, too" (Phil. 2:3–4).

Journal Your Thoughts

Day 107

Prayer for Widows

Dear Father,

I pray for those whose spouses have passed away and who are now alone in the world. Life has changed drastically for them, and I pray for comfort and peace to wash over them abundantly. I pray that they would look to you to meet all of their needs. You have not deserted them. You love them dearly.

When they are alone and the house is quiet, may their memories serve them and warm their hearts. As they fix dinner for one rather than two, bless them with a steadfast heart. If they come across something that was handled by their spouse in the past—something they have never had to do before but must now do themselves—I pray that they would not be crushed, but served. Send them someone to help or direct them to get it done.

I pray for all the widows as they learn to live alone. It is so hard on them, and it is so difficult to have peace at this time. Their hearts are broken, and they can't see the future being bright for them. I pray that you would give them insight into the possibilities of their life after the death of a deeply beloved spouse. Encourage them with your Holy Spirit.

In Jesus' name I pray, amen.

"Father to the fatherless, defender of widows—this is God, whose dwelling is holy" (Psalm 68:5).

Journal Your Thoughts

Day 108

Prayer for Being Still

Dear Jesus,

Sometimes the busyness of each day can overtake me. I feel as if there aren't enough hours in the day to do what needs to be done. I repent of being so busy that I don't have time for you. Forgive me.

Help me to be still before you, knowing that you are God. I pray that I would reprioritize my schedule so that I can spend more time in your presence, meditating on your Word and worshipping you. I ask that my worries and stress would not overtake or overwhelm me. You are in control, and I am not. In the end, all that really matters is my relationship with you. Everything else is secondary. I want to be like Mary, sitting at your feet in quiet admiration even as there are so many other things trying to grab my attention.

I pray for others who have this same struggle. Teach them what it means to be still before you. Help them to carve out the needed time for what matters most. Replace their restless "doing" with your peace. Remind them of your constant, loving presence.

In Jesus' name I pray, amen.

"As Jesus and the disciples continued on their way to Jerusalem, they came to a certain village where a woman named Martha welcomed him into her home. Her sister, Mary, sat at the Lord's feet, listening to what he taught. But Martha was distracted by the big dinner she was preparing. She came to Jesus and said, 'Lord, doesn't it seem unfair to you that my sister just sits here while I do all the work? Tell her to come and help me.' But the Lord

said to her, 'My dear Martha, you are worried and upset over all these details! There is only one thing worth being concerned about. Mary has discovered it, and it will not be taken away from her'" (Luke 10:38–42).

Journal Your Thoughts

Day 109

Prayer for the Poor and Lost

Dear Heavenly Father,

I love how you care for your children, bringing each detail of their needs to your mind. You love each person so much that you want them to learn your ways of caring for one another. Many hearts are broken, even now, over conditions of the heart, finances, homelessness, and relationships. There are so many needs, but you have many ambassadors to be your hands and feet to them.

I pray that I could be a healer and help reconcile people to you. Thank you for gifting me perfectly to do what you have planned for me. I pray that my faith would be strong as I go forth and, in your name, serve those who need hope so badly.

To the poor, I pray encouragement through blessings. The blessings are carried inside each of us, and we can bestow them to others through our deeds and words. I pray for the people who have no place to call home. They are wandering in the world and may feel weak or insignificant. May they be strengthened by others who bring them your love. For those who are hurt in other ways, and perhaps feel angry, bitter, devastated, or lonely, I pray comfort on their hearts, knowing that Jesus is the Lord of lords and loves them with an everlasting love.

In Jesus' name I pray, amen.

"Do not withhold good from those who deserve it when it's in your power to help them. If you can help your neighbor now, don't say, 'Come back tomorrow, and then I'll help you'" (Prov. 3:27–28).

Journal Your Thoughts

Day 110

Prayer for Extending Forgiveness

Dear Almighty God,

Forgiveness is hard to understand. I try to grasp what it really means and how I can extend it to those who have wounded me, but I always seem to fall short. I pray, Lord, for the strength to forgive as a manifestation of how you have forgiven me.

I choose to extend forgiveness to _____ for the offenses of _____, and I no longer want to hold on to bitterness. I trust you, Lord, for whatever comes as a result. I place my hurt and the offenses committed against me into your hands. Thank you that I no longer have to worry about them. I can walk freely in your grace.

I want to be like the father of the prodigal son, who welcomed his wayward child with open arms and an open heart. There was no bitterness in the father's heart, just thankfulness that his son had returned. If the father had not forgiven his son, the ending of the story would have been very different. I do not want to be like the older brother, who held on to anger and jealousy. He felt his brother didn't deserve such rich grace. Perhaps he didn't, but neither do I, Lord.

Let your amazing grace flow through me, dear Lord. Thank you that your grace is limitless, and because of that grace, I can extend grace and forgiveness to others. I pray that others in my life would exercise forgiveness as well.

In Jesus' name I pray, amen.

"Since God chose you to be the holy people he loves, you must clothe yourselves with tenderhearted mercy, kindness, humility, gentleness, and patience. Make

allowance for each other's faults, and forgive anyone who offends you. Remember, the Lord forgave you, so you must forgive others" (Col. 3:12–13).

Journal Your Thoughts

Day 111

Prayer for God's Forgiveness

Dear Lord,

You have held your arms open wide to demonstrate how much you love me and forgave me. On the cross, you took the nails and died so that I would not be separated from you. This is a wonderful and incomprehensible gift. This knowledge is beyond my understanding.

In life, when I have done wrong, there is a price to pay. The guilt I feel for sin holds me back from freely serving you. I feel so badly, Lord, that I have hurt you by my wrongdoing. When I know that I have wronged you, the one who has loved me beyond comprehension, I feel that I am an utter failure. Help me to freely accept your grace. I know that you want me to be released from shame. You freely forgive, but accepting your forgiveness is my choice.

Father, please forgive me for _____. I repent of that sin and agree to commit to the direction that I must go.

You have removed my sins as far as the east is from the west. You do not hold on to my sins, but cast them into the sea of your forgetfulness. You have set me free, and I praise your holy name.

In Jesus' name I pray, amen.

"If we claim we have no sin, we are only fooling ourselves and not living in the truth. But if we confess our sins to him, he is faithful and just to forgive us our sins and to cleanse us from all wickedness" (1 John 1:8–9).

Journal Your Thoughts

Day 112

Prayer for Strength to Forgive Others

Dear Almighty God,

There are times when I don't think I can forgive others because of what they have said or done. I think the hurt they have caused is too great. But I am wrong. Whether the offense was against me or someone else, it is not for me to withhold forgiveness. Your Son took all the sin in my life and put it on himself when he hung on the cross. He did that for me, and I have no right to hold anything against anyone.

What is the cost of my forgiveness? There is no cost; it is priceless. I am choosing to loosen my hold on my right to hang on to hurt and give it to you, Lord. I trust you with my hurts. I see only from my limited perspective, but you know each situation completely and see the whole picture. I give those troubles to you.

I no longer want to offend you, God, by not forgiving. I want to be free, so I choose to extend forgiveness in my heart to people like _____ who have hurt me by _____. Whether the hurt is big or small in my eyes, it's sin for me to hold a grudge. I choose to hold nothing against those who have hurt me. I place those sins in your hands, Jesus.

On the cross you prayed, "Father, forgive them, for they know not what they do." It's true, Lord. None of us sees completely how our actions affect others. I know that you see and know everything, and I am thankful.

In Jesus' name I pray, amen.

"Do not judge others, and you will not be judged. Do not condemn others, or it will all come back against you. Forgive others, and you will be forgiven" (Luke 6:37).

Journal Your Thoughts

Day 113

Prayer for Purity

Dear Precious Lord,

What does it mean to be pure? In your Word, I read that it means to be clean in heart, mind, and soul. How can I be pure before you?

The work that your Son, Jesus, does in my heart cleanses me. I must in obedience give him permission to move in my life in order for me to be pure. I desire purity because that will mean I am closer to you and more like you. Draw me close, Lord. Purge the evil from my heart so that I can be clean before you.

The evidence of a damaged world is everywhere—on the newsstands, on television, and online. I pray that I would stay focused on you and shine your light on anything that is impure. Help me to resist the devil, flee from sin, and turn to you. Darkness cannot stand light, and for us to be pure, the darkness must be cast out.

Lord, I pray for those who think purity is something they cannot attain. With you, nothing is impossible.

Lord, give me your eyes to see, your heart to feel, and your conquering power over sin.

In Jesus' name I pray, amen.

"God blesses those whose hearts are pure for they will see God" (Matt. 5:8).

Journal Your Thoughts

Day 114

Prayer for a Clean Heart

Dear Precious Lord,

"Create in Me a Clean Heart, O God." This is a song I have sung many times. But is it something I really crave for myself? To truly be pure in heart, I must rid myself of the desire to hang on to old habits. This is not always easy, and if I'm honest, it's not something I always want to do. However, it is worth it, for being pure means being closer to you, dear Lord.

To be clean before you, I must keep my constant focus on you. I must also have a desire to remain pure in heart and mind. The world flings at us evil and impurity for our eyes to see and ears to hear. Sometimes it seems impossible not to be infected by such things, but when we are tempted, you always give us a way out. It's a promise in your Word.

I pray for those who are so tied up in worldly things that they have trouble seeing you. This is not because of what you have done, but because of their choices. Lord, I pray that you would break through all of those hindrances and make yourself known to them again and show how much you love them. Thank you, Lord, that you never give up on us. Amen!

"Create in me a clean heart, O God. Renew a loyal spirit within me. Do not banish me from your presence, and don't take your Holy Spirit from me. Restore to me the joy of your salvation, and make me willing to obey you"
(Psalm 51:10–12).

Journal Your Thoughts

Day 115

Prayer to Have Pure Motives

Dear Lord,

I pray that no matter what I do, my motives would be pure. Too often, I allow a self-serving attitude to creep in, and I find myself once again putting myself on the throne instead of you. You deserve to be on the throne of my life at all times. Forgive me when I put myself there instead. Thank you for your grace and mercy when I fail you.

I pray for those whose motives don't always align with being honest and serving others. I pray that their eyes would be opened to what you have in store for them, which is so much greater than what they can achieve on their own. Help them, Lord, to rely on you.

What will my motives be today? I pray that you would examine my motives and help me discern them before taking any action. If I start to become self-serving, prick my conscience, Lord, and stop me in my tracks. Turn me around so that I can once again be walking with you with a pure heart and mind. I wish to glorify you in all I do. Transform my mind, Jesus, to be like yours. That is my heart's desire.

In Jesus' name I pray, amen.

"People may be right in their own eyes, but the Lord examines their heart" (Prov. 21:2).

Journal Your Thoughts

Day 116

Prayer for Greater Faith

Dear Lord,

I pray for my faith to be greater. Sometimes it feels so small. Especially when problems are ongoing, my faith can feel nonexistent. Some days, there seems to be no way out. However, you promise that there is *always* a way out, and that way is discovered through prayer. I pray that I would seek you through this tough journey and grow my faith in you. You have all the blessings in your hand. I desire to obey you in what you show me.

I am so grateful that I don't need to have great faith in order to please you. You say that I only need faith as large as a mustard seed.

I pray for anyone whose faith is wavering right now. I pray that they would see your hand in action in response to their prayers and the prayers of others. I pray that they would remember that your strength, not their own human frailty, is the great foundation of their faith and that you will never leave them.

I pray for faith-forming assignments from you so that I can be stronger in my faith and help others grow in theirs. It is hard to understand how anyone can get through hard times without you. You are so powerful and loving that you can help anyone. You know the bigger picture, Lord, and I pray in to that picture that your will would be done and your name would be glorified.

In Jesus' name I pray, amen.

"You don't have enough faith,' Jesus told them. 'I tell you the truth, if you had faith even as small as a mustard seed, you could say to this mountain, "Move from here to there," and it would move. Nothing would be impossible"' (Matt. 17:20).

Journal Your Thoughts

Day 117

Prayer for Putting God First

Dear Heavenly Father,

You deserve to come first in my life. However, I often find myself sitting on the throne rather than before it. I pray that I would repent of my desire to put myself in your place and joyfully put you back where you belong. You have always gone before me, even when I didn't realize it. You have control over all creation, yet my human heart is deceived into thinking that I deserve more than you've given me. In reality, you have given me more than I deserve.

Lord, I pray for other believers who put worldly things before you. No matter who we are, sometimes we put you last in our hearts. There are so many temptations and distractions that lure us away from you, and the enemy is behind most—if not all—of them. I pray for our eyes to be opened so that we can be aware of the evil of these temptations and turn our backs to it. May our eyes always be focused on you.

It is so good for us to put you first. You know the perfect way we should live. If we simply follow and obey you, we will be where you want us to be. That's why it is a blessing to put you first.

In Jesus' name I pray, amen.

"Seek the Kingdom of God above all else, and live righteously, and he will give you everything you need"
(Matt. 6:33).

Journal Your Thoughts

Day 118

Prayer for Putting on the Full Armor of God

Dear Lord,

We need your protection. Every day, you invite us to put on the full armor of God. If we don't, we are defenseless against the arrows of the enemy. I pray for the protection of my heart and mind, and that you provide the helmet of salvation and the breastplate of righteousness to secure them. I add the belt of truth and the footwear of peace to go forth and share the gospel. Thank you.

I pray for those who do not protect themselves and have allowed Satan to have a foothold in their lives. I pray that they would break free from his grip and use their spiritual armor to protect them from attacks. Their hearts are broken by life's challenges, and they need to be renewed. Lord, I ask that you send someone to encourage and pray for them. You are the resource of everything—your arm is not too short. You can fulfill all that aligns with your will.

Spiritual battle is part of the Christian life. There is no way around it. As soldiers for Christ, I pray that we would fulfill our responsibility to be as equipped as possible for whatever befalls us during the journey.

In Jesus' name I pray, amen.

"For we are not fighting against flesh-and-blood enemies, but against evil rulers and authorities of the unseen world, against mighty powers in this dark world, and against evil spirits in the heavenly places. Therefore, put on every piece of God's armor so you will be able to resist the enemy in the time of evil. Then after the battle you

will still be standing firm. Stand your ground, putting on the belt of truth and the body armor of God's righteousness. For shoes, put on the peace that comes from the Good News so that you will be fully prepared. In addition to all of these, hold up the shield of faith to stop the fiery arrows of the devil. Put on salvation as your helmet, and take the sword of the Spirit, which is the word of God. Pray in the Spirit at all times and on every occasion. Stay alert and be persistent in your prayers for all believers everywhere" (Eph. 6:12–18).

Journal Your Thoughts

Day 119

Prayer for Discerning God's Will

Dear Lord,

How many times have I asked to find your will, only to discover that I wasn't where you wanted me to be? Your will is always being played out, no matter what choices we make. You work through our choices and help us find the better way to live. I pray into that, Lord, and ask that you reveal to me the way I should go in all things. I will listen and obey.

I pray for those who do not know your will and don't want to do so. They are trying to live their own way. Help them to see that your way is the best and only way. Work in their hearts to show them your great love and plan for them.

I also pray for those who want to find your will, but who are frustrated in trying to do so. Give them patience. They might pray, but they don't seem to hear an answer. Maybe they want to give up, but part of the spiritual maturing process is to persevere and keep going. You do have an answer for them and will provide it at just the right time. I pray that they would have the patience and perseverance to keep seeking you.

Your will is all around us, and I pray that we would grasp on to it and join you in what you are doing as you call us. That is your will for us … your perfect will.

In Jesus' name I pray, amen.

"Now may the God of peace—who brought up from the dead our Lord Jesus, the great Shepherd of the sheep, and ratified an eternal covenant with his blood—may he equip you with all you need for doing his will. May he produce in you, through the power of Jesus Christ, every

good thing that is pleasing to him. All glory to him forever and ever! Amen" (Heb. 13:20-21).

Journal Your Thoughts

Day 120

Prayer of Thankfulness for God's Word

Dear Lord,

Your Word lights up the path I am to take, and I thank you for the provision of the Bible. I know you had us in mind when you inspired your servants to put down on paper what you want us to know. Open my eyes to the truths in the Bible so that I might apply them to my life. I am encouraged each day by reading the Scriptures and knowing that you have a plan for me.

I pray for those who have not been reading your Word and feel lost. I pray that you would give them new energy to pick up their Bibles and immerse themselves in the daily bread. This will give them great hope and insight into all you have for them, so I pray for that to come to be.

Your Word is a manual for life. Every human experience is recorded in the Bible, and we can count on the truth of your words to guide us safely through all of our challenges and fears. There is so much wisdom in your Word, and I thank you for sharing it with us so that we might live a victorious life.

In Jesus' name I pray, amen.

"Your word is a lamp to guide my feet and a light for my path" (Psalm 119:105).

Journal Your Thoughts

Day 121

Prayer for Spiritual Growth

Dear Lord,

As parents love to watch their children grow and mature, so you, Lord, love to watch your children mature as strong Christians. To do this, you have given us everything we need. Help us to take advantage of the opportunities to grow and not leave those opportunities for someone else.

Spiritual growth takes place mostly through the challenges in life, so thank you for the struggles I experience so that I can become strong. I pray for insight as I work through difficulties in order to honor and glorify you. I pray for those who desire more spiritual growth. Reveal ways for them to grow in you.

I pray for those who aren't growing spiritually. Lord, I know you love them more than I can imagine and want to see them blossom in you. I pray that you would work on their hearts to become open to the ways they can grow. You can use anything—missions, mentoring, or how they manage their finances—but regardless the challenges you choose, you have planned a perfect path for them. You will take them gently by the hand and guide them. Your call is clear for them. Thank you!

In Jesus' name I pray, amen.

"I am certain that God, who began the good work within you, will continue his work until it is finally finished on the day when Christ Jesus returns" (Phil. 1:6).

Journal Your Thoughts

Day 122

Prayer Against Entitlement

Dear Jehovah Jireh,

So often we get caught up in what you can do for us rather than what we can do for you. I pray for a spirit of humility upon all who struggle with this.

Even when good things happen, it's not because of anything we have done. We don't earn it. We don't deserve it. Good things happen because you are good. We have no claim over the good that is done. Our job is simply to thank you.

I pray for those who are focused on what they, themselves, have accomplished and forget that they can do nothing without you. Instead of making worship of you a priority, they work for the accolades they receive on earth. Give them eyes to see their wrong thinking and help them to give you all the glory—as you deserve.

I pray that in all things I can be humble, knowing that all things come from you. You are Jehovah Jireh, the Provider. Never has there been a day that you have not taken care of me. You are the reason I rise up in the morning, the reason I am able to go about my day, and the reason I can lie down at night. You are always there. I lack nothing that I truly need.

May I never forget that you are the center of my being and my reason for living. May I desire to honor you in all that I do. In all things, may I never fail to give you praise.

In your name I pray, amen.

"He must become greater and greater, and I must become less and less" (John 3:30).

Journal Your Thoughts

Day 123

Prayer for Obedience

Dear Lord,

Why is it that I constantly want to disobey you and obey my natural yearnings instead? Your way is always better, and I know that. I've tested you, and you have been faithful. You say that those who obey you love you, and I want to show my love for you by obeying as I should. Give me your strength to make this happen.

Making choices is always difficult when the world tempts us to choose its way. I pray that we do not fall into this temptation, but rather obey what is truth. You have given us instruction on how to walk in truth and how to repent from walking wrongly. You forgive our bad choices and want us to grow with you and see the Promised Land. We are not alone in this. The Israelites had a problem in doing what they should, as well. Yet, you still love them. You love us, too. Too often, I think I know better, but I don't. I need you to guide me.

I pray for those who have been disobedient and find themselves in trouble. Lord, I ask that you transform their hearts from ones of stone to ones of flesh. I pray that they would see you through the process and be ready to turn away from their old ways and return to following you.

In Jesus' name I pray, amen.

"So I say, let the Holy Spirit guide your lives. Then you won't be doing what your sinful nature craves"
(Gal. 5:16).

Journal Your Thoughts

Day 124

Prayer for Praying More Effectively

Dear Lord,

Thank you for the gift of prayer. You have supplied me with a way to have direct communication with you at any time of day or night. You are always on call. Lord, this wonderful gift is sometimes taken for granted, and I know that I have been guilty of this. Forgive me for my shallowness when I don't put my heart into praying. You meant for it to be so much more.

The power is with you, and if I can tap into your Holy Spirit power, I know that your kingdom will be blessed and expanded. I ask, Lord, for you to give me a heart for going deeper in prayer with you. Please give me opportunities to enrich my prayer life and learn more. I praise you for your goodness in this. I want to approach your throne without fear and to lay myself before you.

I pray for those who seem to have lost the passion for prayer. I pray that you reignite that passion in their hearts and give them a surge of desire for spiritual things. Perhaps we can sharpen one another in this area. If that is your desire, Lord, I pray that it would be so.

In Jesus' name I pray, amen.

"In those days when you pray, I will listen" (Jer. 29:12).

Journal Your Thoughts

Day 125

Prayer for Living in the Present

Dear Lord,

It seems that life long ago was so much better than today. I sometimes want to return to the old ways of doing things, for I feel more comfortable in them. The world has changed so quickly, and I feel as if I'm getting lost in all the changes. I pray for a spirit of discernment in how to handle this. Please equip me with a heart to journey through the "now" rather than the past.

I pray for those who have also struggled with living in the present, for they feel as if their best years are behind them. They look at the world today and see only bad. I know there is so much good that you have planned for them, and I ask for their eyes to be opened to what you have in store. May they open the gifts with gladness and joyful hearts. May they be excited to share the blessings that you give them.

This is not the end of the story, but only the middle. Each day offers a new beginning. You have created a wonderful world for us, and there is still so much of the story to be written. I ask that you remind me that I can live for you in wonderful ways—today—for you are my God, and you never change.

In Jesus' name I pray, amen.

"Yet God has made everything beautiful for its own time. He has planted eternity in the human heart, but even so, people cannot see the whole scope of God's work from beginning to end" (Eccl. 3:11).

Journal Your Thoughts

Day 126

Prayer for Guidance and Direction

Dear Jesus,

Life offers me many paths to take, and finding the right way can be confusing. I pray that I would always be able to look for and find you in every step I take. You have never led me astray, and I truly love to see the adventures on which you take me. Your path is straight. There are no deceiving curves or cliffs. The path is well lit and flat for safe walking. You being the guide helps us travel in peace through the chaos of the world. In all places, there are temptations of evil. Holy Spirit, I pray that you would steer us all clear of that.

I pray for those who are having a difficult time knowing which way to go in their lives. I pray that they would look to you and search your Word for direction. I pray they would not seek the world's opinion, for in doing so, they will be surely led astray.

I pray that you would send someone to help point them in your way. The words of a true friend can act as a calming balm on their minds and hearts. Encouragement from fellow brothers and sisters is needed for everyone. Doing this consciously helps in the growing of their faith. It is all orchestrated by you, Jesus.

I pray this in your precious name, amen.

"The Lord says, 'I will guide you along the best pathway for your life. I will advise you and watch over you'"
(Psalm 32:8).

Journal Your Thoughts

Day 127

Prayer for Those Dealing with Guilt and Shame

Dear Lord,

You never meant for your people to carry guilt and shame. You have made a way for them to be free. I pray that this truth would fill the hearts and minds of all people. I pray for the hurt they are experiencing, whether it is the result of their own choices or not. Your grace covers all. Nothing is beyond your grace.

I pray for those who are suffering from guilt and shame from their pasts. Lord, I pray that you would encourage them and strengthen them. Your children do not need to carry these things any longer. Your cross took care of it for them. If it is your will, use me to help them with words or actions with the goal of drawing them closer to you.

Guilt and shame are footholds, and I pray protection over your people from Satan's tactics to entrap them. Give them wisdom to see the evil at hand and to stay away from it. Guilt and shame can do a lot of damage inside a person's soul. I pray protection over that.

I pray that we would live free from guilt and shame in obedience to you. Let your light shine brightly in our lives.

In Jesus' name I pray, amen.

"Finally, I confessed all my sins to you and stopped trying to hide my guilt. I said to myself, 'I will confess my rebellion to the Lord.' And you forgave me! All my guilt is gone" (Psalm 32:5).

Journal Your Thoughts

Day 128

Prayer for Those Who Struggle with Jealousy

Dear Lord,

That green-eyed monster comes into our lives so unexpectedly and moves right in. One moment, we feel content. The next, we are shown something that makes us forget this contentment and churn up discontentment by turning our focus into what we want and don't have. I pray against this stronghold in people's lives as it causes them to sin and separate from you. By turning our focus once again on you— and only you—this will diminish the jealousy in our hearts.

I pray for those who feel that life is unfair because they do not have what another has. I pray that they would see beyond their own needs and desires and, instead, turn their focus to the hope you have for them. I pray that you would surround them with people with contentment so attractive that they want to experience that contentment for themselves.

Lord, your plans for them are huge. I pray that those who feel "green" towards others will recognize and embrace the opportunities you bring them to move towards a place of contentment. I pray that they would stand strong against the devil. You are hope, Lord.

In your name I pray, amen.

"For wherever there is jealousy and selfish ambition, there you will find disorder and evil of every kind" (James 3:16).

Journal Your Thoughts

Day 129

Prayer for Those Who Struggle with Lust

Dear Heavenly Father,

In your Word, you provide us with many helps to control our lusts. I pray that those struggling with this temptation would take those directions to heart so they would not fall into sin.

I pray that people would see that your commands regarding lust are to help them and not to hurt them. You are providing the best for them in life, and I pray that they would understand this as they struggle. Keep them strong, Lord. The result of giving in to this sin is not only devastating to themselves, but also to others. The wound is deep and hurtful, leaving scars on the souls of those hurt by the one who fell.

I pray for those who are struggling with lust right now, whose bodies are telling them to move ahead and fulfill their sexual desires. I pray for your protection over them. Open the eyes of their hearts so that they would recognize and turn away from the mistakes they could make. May they see your great purpose for them and rip off the blinders put on their eyes by the evil one. The world says that they deserve it, but that's a lie. I pray that your truth would break through any lie they are tempted to believe. I ask for you to bring them out of this darkness.

For those who have fallen into sin from lust, I pray that they would be repentant and that brothers and sisters in the faith would come around them to restore them once again. I pray for mentors to encourage them along this journey and help them to see the right choices to make in the future.

In your precious name I pray, amen.

"The temptations in your life are no different from what others experience. And God is faithful. He will not allow

the temptation to be more than you can stand. When you are tempted, he will show you a way out so that you can endure" (1 Cor. 10:13).

Journal Your Thoughts

Day 130

Prayer for Those Who Need God's Grace and Mercy

Dear Lord,

I pray for your grace and mercy to cover the people you have created and love so much. I pray that rivers of your love would sweep them off their feet and bring them to a place of peace and joy. Their lives may seem like stormy waters, but with a word you can calm the waves. Your Word brings the storms into obedience.

Lord, I pray for anyone who feels alone after making a costly mistake. They are discouraged in their belief that they are being disowned by those they love, that their integrity can never be rebuilt, and that they have no place to go. I pray that those lies would dissolve in the presence of your Word. You lay claim over their souls and will not allow anyone else to take them. They are yours alone.

I pray for people who need to show grace and mercy to others. May that be their first response and not an afterthought. I pray that they would be intentional in showing your love to those who have fallen short. No one should cast the first stone, for we all have fallen short and need your mercy and forgiveness.

In Jesus' name I pray, amen!

"So let us come boldly to the throne of our gracious God. There we will receive his mercy, and we will find grace to help us when we need it most" (Heb. 4:16).

Journal Your Thoughts

Day 131

Prayer for Those Who Feel Weak

Dear Lord,

In your midst are people who feel powerless and weak. I pray that from the center of their core, they would gain strength in knowing they belong to you. Strength does not come from their actions, but from their obedience. You love them for who they are—just as they are—right now. I pray that they would see you at work in their lives because it is in their weakness that your glory can be seen.

I pray for those who have low self-esteem. They believe that everyone else is stronger than they are and capable of so much. These individuals have great potential because of you. Your plans for their lives are rich, and I pray they would not sell out to the world and believe its lies about what a strong person is and is not.

Your plan for each one of us is to be dependent on you so that we can rely on your power and not on our own. I pray that truth would fill the minds and hearts of those discouraged by feeling "less than" when the truth is that their value and worth is infinite.

In Jesus' name I pray, amen.

"Each time he said, 'My grace is all you need. My power works best in weakness.' So now I am glad to boast about my weaknesses, so that the power of Christ can work through me. That's why I take pleasure in my weaknesses, and in the insults, hardships, persecutions, and troubles that I suffer for Christ. For when I am weak, then I am strong" (2 Cor. 12:9–10).

Journal Your Thoughts

Day 132

Prayer for Godly Character

Dear Father,

Our character is to be a reflection of yours. At times, we all struggle to follow your model of what it means to be a man or woman of character. Our character is one of the most important aspects of who we are in you. Our character reflects what we believe and whether we can be trusted. If our character is tarnished, it does not build back up quickly or easily, and it can be a painful process. May we not give in to our flesh in any way. In all ways, may we reflect your love and character.

I pray for those whose character has been more defined by serving the world than serving you. I pray that they would see the futility of this path and turn their backs on it. I pray they would be enlightened to your way of living and be obedient in following it. Their lives will become more meaningful as they focus on their purpose in you and not on the lure of the world.

Lord, I ask that you examine my character and use the Holy Spirit to point out where I need to change. My faults are many, I know, and you have a better way planned for me. May I grow strong in character and be a leader who encourages others how to grow in this manner, as well.

In Jesus' name I pray, amen.

"We can rejoice, too, when we run into problems and trials, for we know that they help us develop endurance. And endurance develops strength of character, and character strengthens our confident hope of salvation. And this hope will not lead to disappointment. For we

know how dearly God loves us, because he has given us the Holy Spirit to fill our hearts with his love" (Rom. 5:3–5).

Journal Your Thoughts

Day 133

Prayer for Those Whose Trials Seem Unending

Dear Lord,

You know how hard it is to climb one mountain only to see another one right after it. Trials sometimes feel as if they are insurmountable mountains, but moving mountains is not difficult for you. I pray for strength to continue when it seems as if I am getting nowhere. I pray, Lord, that you would lift me above my troubles so that I can see only you. You—not my problems—are where I need to focus.

Jesus, I bring all before you who are struggling day after day with trials that seem to have no end. Things may get a little better one day, and the next day they seem right back to where they were. Help these people, dear Lord. Help them overcome adversity and triumph over the worldly spiral of this situation. I ask for people to come around them to encourage and strengthen their sense of self. In your eyes, they are more than their problems. Their problems don't define them—you do.

Holy Spirit, I ask that you reign in the hearts of those who are downtrodden. Help them to let go of their baggage and raise their hands in worship to you. Heal their minds and spirits so they can see the great plan you have for them. Their race is not finished.

In Jesus' name I pray, amen.

"Rejoice in our confident hope. Be patient in trouble, and keep on praying" (Rom. 12:12).

Journal Your Thoughts

Day 134

Prayer for Positive Thinking of Others

Dear Lord,

It's easy to be discouraged by people and to become judgmental. I pray that I would be able to see the good things in people for I want them to see the good things in me. Loving my neighbor is more than bringing cookies to the family next door. It is bringing those people before you in prayer.

I need to love others as I want to be loved. This includes people who are different from me, who might even make me uncomfortable. Help me to think encouraging thoughts about them.

I pray for those who are struggling with thinking good things about certain people in their lives. Maybe these are people with whom they have had conflict in the past or who hold different opinions than they do. Open their eyes, Lord, to how you see these people. Help them to grasp the importance of seeing people through your eyes and loving them the way you do.

Each day brings a new opportunity to love our neighbor and think positive things about them. Each person has great value to you, and you do not want us to say or think negative things about them. May our thoughts reflect your thoughts. Help us see people the way you do. Remind us that even people we don't like can be used by you for our good.

In Jesus' name I pray, amen.

"A second is equally important: 'Love your neighbor as yourself'" (Matt. 22:39).

Journal Your Thoughts

Day 135

Prayer Against Gossip

Dear Lord,

Our tongues are gifts from you. We can use our tongues to build people up or to tear them down. When we use our tongues to gossip, we are using your gift as a tool of destruction. We do not have the authority to condemn another child of yours.

Lord, I pray against anyone who feels that they have the right to gossip about another. You have called your people to build one another up. Gossip destroys. I pray for the equipping of your people by your Holy Spirit to boldly not allow gossip to creep into their midst.

I pray for those who struggle with gossip. I pray that they would see the error of their ways. Convict their hearts so that they would tame their tongues and use them to provide encouraging words that build up others instead.

Protect the churches, Lord, as they sometimes confuse gossip with prayer requests. Help them to discern what is properly a prayer request and what is not. Thank you for your Word that clearly instructs us on how to speak to one another. Following a worldly doctrine will only bring pain. Where gossip has caused destruction, I pray for forgiveness, healing, and restoration.

In your precious and holy name, I pray, amen.

"The tongue can bring death or life; those who love to talk will reap the consequences" (Prov. 18:21).

Journal Your Thoughts

Day 136

Prayer for Being Responsive to God's Leading

Dear Jesus,

How many times has your Spirit nudged me to do something and I ignored those promptings? Forgive me when I have not obeyed. I pray for the courage and strength to do every task you give me. I pray that each time I feel those promptings, I would say, "Here I am, Lord." I want to be a good and faithful servant.

I lift up those who feel discouraged by not hearing your voice. Encourage them in ways that would allow them to hear your voice and respond. I also pray for your Spirit to search their hearts for anything that might be a barrier between them and you. Holy Spirit, break through any walls that prevent them from hearing your voice. Allow your words to permeate their minds and souls so that they know you are at work in them.

I pray for those who are struggling with not obeying the whispers you are putting in their hearts. May they find that you are their strong foundation and will not allow them to fall. May their inner core become strong so they can move ahead with choices that will bring you honor and glory.

Thank you for working in our lives as we seek to be the hands and feet of Jesus. We are Jesus with skin on, and it is a clear way we are to minister to others.

It's all by your power, amen.

"If you love me, obey my commandments" (John 14:15).

Journal Your Thoughts

Day 137

Prayer for Courage

Dear Lord,

I pray for a heart that is free from fear in serving you. So many things in this world create fear, but your power dispels it. I want a heart like that of David, who was not afraid of Goliath and who stepped forward with no fear because of what he believed about you. You have never let me down, so I can trust you with everything.

I pray for those who are filled with fear and who truly need courage to journey through their situations. I pray that the presence of the Holy Spirit would come over them and empower them to move ahead. I pray for your mercy and grace in their lives and that they would see your hand at work.

Thank you for the many examples of courage throughout the Bible. I am encouraged by the stories of the men and women who displayed total trust in you. They are models for me and others. The truths in your Word are there to encourage us to do likewise. I pray that as a nation, we would do that. I pray that we would throw fear out the window rather than allow it to remain in the passenger seats as we travel along our journeys. You are the one with all the power. Amen.

"So be strong and courageous! Do not be afraid and do not panic before them. For the Lord your God will personally go ahead of you. He will neither fail you nor abandon you" (Deut. 31:6).

Journal Your Thoughts

Day 138

Prayer for Contentment

Dear Lord,

You have given me so much. Thank you for your provision and the lavish way you show your love to me. Even with all that, at times I want more. I believe the lie that something is lacking in my life. Please forgive me for falling for that deception. I have all that I need. What I do with it is up to me, and I pray that I would make good choices in handling what you have blessed me with every day.

Lord, I pray for those who are restless and discontent. They feel as if they need more and more to make them feel good about themselves. This is the lie of the world, and the desire to feed this discontentment can become an idol if we allow it to. I pray against any strongholds that prey on your people. The goal of these strongholds is to get our eyes off of you. Idols want our worship, and I pray against all of them.

I pray for the peace of contentment over the lives of people. When we are happy with what we have, it frees us to serve you more, knowing that all things are taken care of by your hand. Can we remember the sparrow and how you keep your eye on it? You do so much more for us. Thank you, dear Jesus!

In your precious name I pray, amen.

"Yet true godliness with contentment is itself great wealth. After all, we brought nothing with us when we came into the world, and we can't take anything with us when we leave it. So if we have enough food and clothing, let us be content" (1 Tim. 6:6–8).

Journal Your Thoughts

Day 139

Prayer for Dwelling in Truth

Dear Jesus,

In this world, we often wonder what is true and what is not. I pray for discernment and wisdom so that our choices will bring you glory. Your truth is what glows brightly in our lives. We can walk in great confidence when walking in truth. You shine truth on our paths so that we will not falter.

Most darkness in this world is caused by the cover-up of your truth. I pray for enlightenment on all evil in the world so that it would be destroyed. Your truth is power. That is what is called "the sword of the Spirit." I pray that I would arm myself with that sword and use it for your purposes.

I pray for those who haven't been listening to or believing your truth. I ask, dear Lord, that you would change their minds and allow truth to transform their lives. I pray that they would see your hand as holding all the power and not the world. What a difference it would make for them to walk in truth rather than darkness. Light is needed to grow in faith, and I pray that they would blossom under your light of truth. Shine brightly, Jesus, so all can see.

In your name I pray, amen.

"You will know the truth, and the truth will set you free"
(John 8:32).

Journal Your Thoughts

Day 140

Prayer for Strength

Dear Lord,

Thank you for being my strong tower. I know that I can count on you to get me through each day. When I feel weak, help me feel your presence more strongly. I know that you will encourage and equip me. You are glorified through my weakness, for any strength I have is from you.

I pray specifically for those who are enduring very difficult times, yet still lean on you and your promises. Continue to work through their lives and help them be models of your strength and goodness. You will not leave them in their time of trouble. You will lift them up in your hand and help them persevere.

You are a mighty God who promises to strengthen those who are yours. If we keep our focus on you, we will be able to see you at work. Dim the cares of the world and allow us to see that you are the most important thing. There is no other above you. I pray that the blinders of the world would fall off the eyes of those who have been cheated into thinking there is more strength in the world than in you. May they see clearly your truth and live it out.

In your name I pray, amen.

"The name of the Lord is a strong fortress; the godly run to him and are safe" (Prov. 18:10).

Journal Your Thoughts

Day 141

Prayer for Patience

Dear Lord,

I think praying for patience is like praying to lose weight. Patience doesn't "just happen." It takes hard work. If we pray for patience, you will often help us become more patient by allowing us to walk through challenges. These challenges give us opportunities to grow so we can gain the patience we seek.

I pray for those who struggle with patience, including me. Patience is a fruit of your Spirit that you have given us, but we must ask ourselves: Have we made use of the fruit or kept it in storage? It's important to display patience to give it an opportunity to grow.

I pray for those who have difficulty exhibiting patience, especially with others. I ask for grace in all of their interactions. May your truth shine bright in their lives so that they can see that they have a role to play in how patient they are in all circumstances. Give them insight into becoming more like you. Help them understand the patience that you show them every day. Love them beyond what they can comprehend because of the patience you have for them.

In Jesus' name I pray, amen.

"The Lord isn't really being slow about his promise, as some people think. No, he is being patient for your sake. He does not want anyone to be destroyed, but wants everyone to repent" (2 Pet. 3:9).

Journal Your Thoughts

Day 142

Prayer for God's Love to Be Evident in Me

Dear Lord,

Throughout your Word, you say that you love me. Thank you for that promise. You not only say the words, but you also back them up with action. You have shown your great love for me every day in all that you provide for me. Every detail in my life is important to you. No one loves me like you do. Believing this gives me strength for each day.

Lord, I ask for your grace for those who suffer because they don't know or understand your love for them. They believe what the world tells them, but in the end, the world only brings false hope and disappointment. May your love wash over them in such a way that there is no denying it. I ask that they would let go of the world's opinion and hang on to your promises alone. Let your love become apparent in their lives.

As I walk with you each day, living out the love you have for me, help me to share that great hope with those around me. I want the world to turn away from its evil and focus on you and your great love. That makes living filled with joy.

Thank you, Jesus, amen.

"May the Lord lead your hearts into a full understanding and expression of the love of God and the patient endurance that comes from Christ" (2 Thess. 3:5).

Journal Your Thoughts

Day 143

Prayer for Faithfulness

Dear Lord,

You are so faithful, and I am not. I desire to be, but in my human condition, I cannot be faithful at all times. I pray for your Spirit to help me become more faithful. I want to do what you call me to do—that is to live in faithfulness. You have been there for me in all things. Your faithfulness is amazing.

I pray for those who are struggling with being faithful in all that they need to do. They have lost sight of their priorities and are focusing on things of the world and not the kingdom. They need your encouragement, Lord, to become faithful. May your Spirit guide and direct them and encourage them into lives of faithfulness.

Faithfulness is a fruit of your Spirit. It is something we already have. It is a gift. I pray that we would allow that gift to do its work so that we might become the faithful people you desire us to be. In doing so, we as your people become the hands and feet of Jesus to others. In our giving and serving, you are glorified in our active faithfulness, for we serve no other master.

In Jesus' name I pray, amen.

"The trustworthy person will get a rich reward, but a person who wants quick riches will get into trouble"
(Prov. 28:20).

Journal Your Thoughts

Day 144

Prayer for Comfort

Dear Jesus,

Life has its "ups" when we are on the mountaintop and everything is great. In these times, we feel that we can celebrate freely. Other times, life has its "downs," when we are living in the valley and our hearts are dark and full of pain.

In these times, it is often hard to find comfort. Sometimes it feels too difficult even to lift our heads. You seem so distant. Is that because you truly are distant? Or because we have pushed you away? You are the God of all comfort and know exactly what each of us needs to feel peace once again.

I pray for those whose sadness is overwhelming and who feel they are beyond consolation. I pray for a wash of your love and peace over them. Send people to them who know how they feel and what to say. May their earthly comfort come from unexpected places. Strengthen them, dear Lord, so they may once again have joy and live out their life in abundance.

I know that your plan for each of us is perfect, and the painful times are not wasted. They have a purpose for your kingdom, and in ways we cannot understand, you use them for our good. The valleys are as important as the mountaintops, and I pray for insight so that I can persevere in my Christian journey and become the person you want me to be.

In Jesus' name I pray, amen.

"All praise to God, the Father of our Lord Jesus Christ. God is our merciful Father and the source of all comfort. He comforts us in all our troubles so that we can comfort others. When they are troubled, we will be able to give them the same comfort God has given us" (2 Cor. 1:3–4).

Journal Your Thoughts

Day 145

Prayer for Blessing

Dear Lord,

You bless me abundantly, and I thank you for that. It sometimes seems odd to ask for blessings, but I believe that is what you would have us do. Perhaps we are to ask for blessings (even when we already have them) so we never forget their true source, which is you. You are ready to bless us, and we are to acknowledge that fact.

In my prayers, it feels strange to focus on myself rather than others, but I pray blessings over my life every day in obedience to you. Thank you for your abundant grace. I want to be like your servant Jabez, who prayed for his territory to be enlarged, for your hand to be on him, and to keep him out of danger. You honor requests for blessings like that.

Father, I pray for blessings on the lives of those who are experiencing difficulties, even at the present moment. I pray that you would bestow on them all they need so that they will be able to give a testimony of your goodness to them. You are so good to us, Lord, and I praise you for that.

In your name I pray, amen.

"He [Jabez] was the one who prayed to the God of Israel, 'Oh, that you would bless me and expand my territory! Please be with me in all that I do, and keep me from all trouble and pain!' And God granted him his request" (1 Chron. 4:10).

Journal Your Thoughts

Day 146

Prayer for Experiencing the Power of God

Dear God,

Your power is infinite. With only a word, you created the world. It's hard to comprehend that kind of power, but I am so glad it is you who holds it. There is no one else to whom to look for help but you . . . and you are good. I praise you for the ways you use your power to help your people. You show me that the world does not have the victory over you, but you have victory over the world. I believe you.

I pray for your power for those who need to be strengthened in the valleys through which they are traveling now. Be their light, O Lord, to guide them along the path. Let them experience your power of discernment and perseverance during this dark time. You have them in your hand and will not let them go.

Empower me, dear Lord, to do your will. Give me eyes to see, ears to hear, and a heart that is open to everything you have for me. Let me experience your power to help the people whom you love. You will not forget them nor me. Thank you!

In Jesus' name I pray, amen.

"During my time here, I protected them by the power of the name you gave me. I guarded them so that not one was lost, except the one headed for destruction, as the Scriptures foretold" (John 17:12).

Journal Your Thoughts

Day 147

Prayer for Giving to God

Dear Father God,

What earthly thing can I give you that has any worth to you? You own all things and have created all things. However, you do ask me to give back a portion of that with which I have been blessed. You bless me to be a blessing to others, but I know that I have struggled with this at times. I pray that I can be obedient in this.

I pray for those who are holding on tightly to everything they have been given and who are fearful of giving back to you. I pray for the grace to see that they don't need to be afraid in their generosity to you, for you are the King of Kings and own it all anyway. You will take care of them in all seasons.

Whether it is time, money, or anything else, I want to be your servant, Lord, and give to you. Help me to loosen my grip on all you have given me and really learn the blessing of giving. Nudge my spirit when you want me to give. Allow me to be used for your glory and not mine. It all comes from you.

In Jesus' name I pray, amen.

"The earth is the Lord's, and everything in it. The world and all its people belong to him" (Psalm 24:1).

Journal Your Thoughts

Day 148

Prayer for Radical Obedience

Dear Lord,

I pray that I would have radical obedience to you. I want to serve you with no excuses. The world taunts me to follow them, but I want my obedience to you to override all temptation. I can do this in your strength. You give me power to withstand all temptations that pull me away from following you.

This is radical obedience. Your way is the best way in all things. I do not need to worry or falter in my choice. You are the clear way to go.

Jesus, give this desire for radical obedience to others. So many are running in all directions trying to find purpose. Help them understand that you—and you alone—are their purpose. You give them the meaning they are searching for. To find purpose, all they have to do is serve you, and they will be right every time. I pray that they would come to understand your truth in their lives.

I pray for a world that wants to be obedient to you. That is your desire. Even though you give us freedom of choice, you are longsuffering in your desire for people to have knowledge of the truth. I pray that, one by one, all people would become everything they can in you by simply being obedient.

In your name I pray, amen.

"The Lord isn't really being slow about his promise, as some people think. No, he is being patient for your sake. He does not want anyone to be destroyed, but wants everyone to repent" (2 Pet. 3:9).

Journal Your Thoughts

Day 149

Prayer for Worshiping God with Everything

Dear Lord,

Do I truly understand what it means to worship you? I pray that your Holy Spirit would guide me in doing so. I want to give you everything. You are so worthy of all praise that I can't help but give you glory.

What gets in the way of me worshiping you fully? The barrier is in me, not you. Maybe I am too busy judging someone or worrying about my own problems. In doing so, I allow these things to get in the way. Help me, Jesus, to put all distractions out of my mind and keep my focus on you.

I pray for the Church, that your servants would focus on what is important and not on what pleases others. You are the only one whom we are to please. Our worship is for you and no one else. Convict the heart of anyone who tries to direct worship away from you. The unity of the body of Christ needs to be in you.

I love to worship you, Lord, and I thank you for your Holy Spirit, who joins in the act of worship. He brings it to a higher level that is a blessing to all. Be glorified in it all, dear Jesus!

In your name I pray, amen.

"But the time is coming—indeed it's here now—when true worshipers will worship the Father in spirit and in truth. The Father is looking for those who will worship him that way" (John 4:23).

Journal Your Thoughts

Day 150

Prayer for Escape from Temptation

Dear Father,

I know that Satan tries to lure me away from you with many pretty and shiny things that catch my eye. I choose how I am going to respond to those things. That is no one else's choice but my own.

You call me to be obedient and to live in obedience. You are glorified in that. The battle for glory occurs when the attacks of the evil one come against me to push me off course. When this happens, I pray for your strength and discernment. Each time that temptation comes, you have promised to show me a way out. Each time, it is my choice to take that way out or not.

I pray for anyone who is being led astray by the lure of the world. Send your people to them to help them escape temptation and see the way they should go. Your plan for them is so much more than what the world can offer them. I pray that they would come to understand that truth and act on it.

Thank you, Lord, for the times you have helped me to escape temptation. I know that the lion lurks around every corner, ready to devour me. But you have protected me so many times. I praise you!

In your name I pray, amen.

"Stay alert! Watch out for your great enemy, the devil. He prowls around like a roaring lion, looking for someone to devour. Stand firm against him, and be strong in your faith. Remember that your family of believers all over the

world is going through the same kind of suffering you are"
(1 Pet. 5:8-9).

Journal Your Thoughts

Day 151

Prayer to Stop Worrying

Dear Abba, Father,

Worry is the temptation for me to try to control my situation. It is also a lack of trust in you. I am commanded not to worry because it places my trust in myself and gives me a false sense of control.

Relying on you, Lord, is so much better. I can trust you with all things in my life because I know of your power and great love for me. This is truth that I stand on. Every time I start to worry, I pray for your grace and mercy to get back on track. I want to trust you with my whole heart.

I pray for those whose lives are filled with worry. I pray for your Holy Spirit to give them discernment and truth. They do not have to worry, for you are caring for them through it all. You want the best for them.

Worry gets me nowhere. Someone once said that trying to fix things by worrying is like trying to get to the store in a rocking chair. I can rock all day long, and I can rock faster and faster and faster, but no matter how much effort I put into rocking, I won't get anywhere. Worrying is not your will for me. Show me in your Word, Lord, the promises I need to remember in order to face any challenge.

In your precious name I pray, amen.

"That is why I tell you not to worry about everyday life—whether you have enough food and drink, or enough clothes to wear. Isn't life more than food, and your body more than clothing? Look at the birds. They don't plant or harvest or store food in barns, for your heavenly

Father feeds them. And aren't you far more valuable to him than they are?" (Matthew 6:25–26).

Journal Your Thoughts

Day 152

Prayer for Disabling Doubt

Dear Lord,

Search my heart for any doubts I may have about you. I consider them sin and want them to be washed away in your cleansing blood. You have already proved who you are, what you can do, who I am in you, and how you make a difference in my life. There is no room for doubt. There is only abundant love and grace.

I pray for those who are struggling with doubt about you right now. May your Spirit override that doubt with truth and may they believe and trust in that truth. Your love for them is overflowing, and you have a plan for them to help them stop doubting. You are working in their lives and showing them the great God that you are.

I pray that I would be a tool used to disable doubt in others. I commit to testifying to what you have done in my life and pray that it would draw others closer to you. I pray against any forces that try to hinder that work and keep doubt alive. Push those forces away, Lord. Allow your holy presence to take over and leave room for doubt no longer.

In your precious and holy name, I pray, amen.

"But when you ask him [for anything], be sure that your faith is in God alone. Do not waver, for a person with divided loyalty is as unsettled as a wave of the sea that is blown and tossed by the wind" (James 1:6).

Journal Your Thoughts

Day 153

Prayer Against Acting Out in Anger

Dear Jesus,

Violence is filling our communities, and I ask for your peace. For many people, violence comes from believing the lies of the world that they need to fight to get ahead. They believe that if anyone does them wrong, they have a right to revenge. These are lies. Your Word tells us that we are yours, and if there is any revenge to be had, it will come from you.

Jesus, I know that Satan uses anger as a tool to get a foothold in our souls, so I pray that you would guide our responses so you get the glory. We do not need to do anything other than what you command. It is good to fight for things like justice and equality, but I pray that we would not sin in the process.

I pray for those who are so angry at people and circumstances that they resort to violence. I pray peace and comfort over their souls so that they would be able to serve you with open arms and not clenched fists. I pray that you would show them that you have control over all things. You do not let any detail pass without your knowledge. You will handle it, and you will be glorified.

In Jesus' name I pray, amen.

"Don't sin by letting anger control you. Don't let the sun go down while you are still angry, for anger gives a foothold to the devil" (Eph. 4:26–27).

Journal Your Thoughts

Day 154

Prayer for Rising Above Discouragement

Dear Jesus,

You know the discouragement I have felt in my heart by trying to do the right thing, only to find that my choices were not your choices. Discouragement seems to come in cycles and is highly effective at taking my focus off of you and putting it on myself. That's when I begin to believe what the evil one says about me and not what you say. You are the only one who can judge me because you created me.

Thank you for the truth found in your Word about who I am and what I mean to you. I am encouraged by your Spirit. You raise me up so that I can once again walk in confidence with you.

I pray for those who are discouraged and not sure which way to turn. I pray that your Holy Spirit would lift them up by sending your people to talk with them about your truth. May they see how you are working in their lives and know that they have purpose. You love them so much and want them to experience your joy in abundance. May your Holy Spirit lavish them with your love.

In Jesus' name I pray, amen.

"This is my command—be strong and courageous! Do not be afraid or discouraged. For the Lord your God is with you wherever you go" (Joshua 1:9).

Journal Your Thoughts

Day 155

Prayer for Releasing Resentment

Dear Heavenly Father,

I may believe that I have no resentment residing in me, but as soon as a name comes up or I see a certain face, I feel the resentment building. I might not want to admit it, but the resentment is there. I pray, Jesus, that you would take it from me. It weighs me down and deters me from what I should be doing for you.

I remember how you responded when people were mocking you, beating you, and spitting on you. I remember how you responded even when they were crucifying you. You said, "Father, forgive them. They know not what they do." Ultimately, the people who have hurt me don't know what they are doing either.

If you, Lord, were treated so badly, why would I think it would be different for me? I pray for the strength to respond in love as you did.

Lord, I pray for those who are holding on to resentment. I pray for a calming of their spirits, that they would experience your peace and grace by releasing their resentment and giving it to you instead. You can handle it. You want to take it from them—and from all of us.

In Jesus' name I pray, amen.

"Look after each other so that none of you fails to receive the grace of God. Watch out that no poisonous root of bitterness grows up to trouble you, corrupting many"
(Heb. 12:15).

Journal Your Thoughts

Day 156

Prayer for Resolving Conflict

Dear Lord,

I pray that I would be used as a tool in resolving conflict in my life as well as in the lives of others. Conflict seems to be a way of life for many, but it doesn't have to be. Give me the desire to see things from someone else's point of view and to show love to the one with whom I am in conflict. This will put me in a place of peace. Conflict tears at relationships, and I don't want to destroy the relationships in my life. I ask for a clear, discerning mind as I journey through a time of conflict.

I pray for those who are experiencing conflict right now. Please give them wisdom as they maneuver their way through this difficult season. May your Holy Spirit carry them through and help them speak words of peace that help diffuse the tension. Show them the better way, dear Lord.

Conflict can be a good thing when it is used to refine us and help us become all we were meant to be. Conflict for its own sake, however, is from the evil one. It is used to divide God's people and get their focus off of you. I pray for a heart that understands the person with whom I am in conflict and that is open as we work through the struggle. May I truly *listen* and not just hear. It is always to your glory.

In Jesus' name I pray, amen.

"A gentle answer deflects anger, but harsh words make tempers flare" (Prov. 15:1).

Journal Your Thoughts

Day 157

Prayer for Being Hospitable

Dear Lord,

You are the model of hospitality. You invite me into your world and provide for me. You love and care for me. You give me purpose and direct my ways. You are the host of my life. Thank you for making me feel welcome, loved, and cared for. I feel so blessed that I want to bless others with a heart to serve.

I pray that my spirit would be in line with yours in being hospitable. Am I welcoming, helping, serving, and loving enough to be a good hostess? Have I served angels unawares? I pray, Lord, that I would always be at my best when it comes to serving others. I want others whom I am serving to see you and not me. Through my hospitality, I pray that they would be drawn closer to you.

I pray for those who might struggle with hospitality. Perhaps they want to do the right thing, but the world holds them back and puts fear into their hearts about what they could lose. Anoint them with your Holy Spirit so that they would see the truth about being hospitable. You desire your people to do this in your name, amen.

"Don't forget to show hospitality to strangers, for some who have done this have entertained angels without realizing it!" (Heb. 13:2).

Journal Your Thoughts

Day 158

Prayer to Have Deeper Compassion

Dear Father,

I see the faces of the homeless, orphans, starving, and downtrodden, and feel so overwhelmed. What can I do to help? I am only one person. Help me to see how you can use me to help others, even if it's one person at a time. I do not have to do it all, only what you direct me to do. That is enough for you, so that is enough for me.

Your plan is perfect, and that is what I am to follow. You said we would always have the hurting among us, so their presence is no surprise to you. I pray that my heart would be moved with compassion for those you want me to serve.

This service of compassion is not only for those who are the most desperate, but also for anyone in need. Lord, help me be sensitive to their circumstances and hurt with them as they suffer. I don't want them to think they are alone, because they are not. They have you and me to care for them.

Lord, please give your people deeper compassion for those who are hurting as a result of the pains of this sinful world. I pray that they would overcome any judgmental attitude and take on your attitude of compassion for others. You care, so that means we are to care, too. You call me to have compassion on others to help them grow in their faith and stand up to evil intent.

In your name I pray, amen.

"Be kind to each other, tenderhearted, forgiving one another, just as God through Christ has forgiven you"
(Eph. 4:32).

Journal Your Thoughts

Day 159

Prayer for Seeing My True Self-Worth

Dear Lord,

I pray that today I can feel my worth in you—worth that is set by you and nobody else. Help me to keep my eyes focused on your love, which has infinite value. I turn my back on the lies of the world. The world and the evil one try to convince me that I am insignificant. I reject those thoughts in your name.

I pray for those who feel that they have no worth at all. They see their lives as a mistake. Lord, I ask your Holy Spirit to come upon them with the truth of your great love for them. Show them the wonderful purpose you have for them and how you will use them for your kingdom.

I praise you, Jesus, for the wonderful work you have done in me in helping me to see who you are and who I am in you. You are my strong foundation, and I stand on you through every struggle. You are my Father, and I am your child. You love me so much that I cannot comprehend it. I love you so much!

In your precious and holy name, I pray, amen.

"I knew you before I formed you in your mother's womb. Before you were born I set you apart and appointed you as my prophet to the nations" (Jer. 1:5).

Journal Your Thoughts

Day 160

Prayer for Setting Good Priorities

Dear Jesus,

My day is planned, or I think it is, but I know that you have a bigger picture in mind that may be different from mine. I pray that I would follow your plan and not my own. I want everything that you have set aside for me today. Your plan is always richer than mine. Today, my first priority is you. Spending time with my dearest friend, Jesus, fills me up so that I can confidently walk through the day. Wash your Spirit over me as I prioritize you.

I pray for those who are struggling with priorities in their lives. They seem to run around putting out fires, getting exhausted and not getting ahead. They feel discouraged, and I believe that you, Lord, can set them on the right track. I know that you love them and know their best priority is you, as well. Help them to see that truth and live it out.

I pray that I would be consistent in my priorities each day, knowing what is truly important. I believe, Jesus, that you gave me the gift of choice so that I could struggle and become stronger in knowing what really matters. I praise you, Lord!

In your name I pray, amen.

"You can make many plans, but the Lord's purpose will prevail" (Prov. 19:21).

Journal Your Thoughts

Day 161

Prayer for Learning from Mistakes

Dear Father God,

I hate to make mistakes. I desire to be perfect, but know that is not possible. Only you are perfect. Thank you for the grace you show me when I stumble. In your mercy, even my mistakes do not go to waste. You always help me to learn a lesson from them. Help me to grasp your wisdom through my mistakes and, in the future, make better choices that honor you.

I pray for those who seem to be stuck because of mistakes they made. Like ships tethered by heavy anchors, they aren't getting ahead through them. Maybe it is because they are not willing to acknowledge that they made bad choices. Maybe it's because they are trying to run from those choices or cover them up. Whatever the reason, shine your light on these mistakes for your good purposes. When we do wrong, we need to see that we have done so, repent from that wrong, and, if possible, try to make it right. Show us, I pray, that there is forgiveness for any offense and that we don't have to hide from you.

Lord, thank you for loving your children who are easily tripped up by the world. Every time we fall, you pick us up, give us a hug, and continue to help us go the right way. Your patience is unending. You never give up on us. Thank you.

In Jesus' name I pray, amen.

"If we confess our sins to him, he is faithful and just to forgive us our sins and to cleanse us from all wickedness" (1 John 1:9).

Journal Your Thoughts

Day 162

Prayer for Dealing with Disappointment

Dear Lord,

I have been disappointed so many times. I know the pain of not getting what I expect from a relationship, a job, my circumstances, or anything else. It hurts, and my emotions tend to dictate my response. But that's not what you want for me. Give me the strength to walk through disappointment and learn to trust you in it. Your plan for me is always best.

Disappointment seems to be overwhelming to so many people today. Encourage them, Lord. I pray that you would use those around them to provide words of encouragement that they can trust you and have hope in your words, Jesus. I pray that they would be given eyes to see and ears to hear the plan you have for them. You will never disappoint them. You are faithful and have the best in mind for them.

There are opportunities and lessons to be learned through disappointment, and I pray that I would grow wiser and stronger because of them. Allow me to experience hard times if they will make me all you want me to be. It's all for your glory.

In Jesus' name I pray, amen.

"We know that God causes everything to work together for the good of those who love God and are called according to his purpose for them" (Rom. 8:28).

Journal Your Thoughts

Day 163

Prayer for Israel

Dear Heavenly Father,

From the beginning, you have had a place in your heart for Israel. They were the first nation to which you committed publicly, and through them, you have allowed all people to be part of your kingdom. I pray against the strife that Israel experiences and ask for peace for that country. This is the land of your covenant, intended to be blessed to be a blessing. May that truth live out for those who live there.

I pray specifically for the war and destruction that happens in Israel. The bloodshed is heartbreaking, and I pray that you, Lord, would be in control and show your power to a hurting country. You have a plan for those people, as well as for us. You promise to bring the Jewish people back to you in your timing. I pray we stay in prayer for that to happen.

I pray that the land would be given to the Jewish people as ordered in the Bible. May nothing stand in the way of their inheritance. They are your holy people, Jesus, and we are to love and support them until the glorious day of your return.

In the name of Jesus, I pray, amen.

"After Lot had gone, the Lord said to Abram, 'Look as far as you can see in every direction—north and south, east and west. I am giving all this land, as far as you can see, to you and your descendants as a permanent possession'"
(Gen. 13:14–15).

Journal Your Thoughts

Day 164

Prayer for Myself and Others Who Have Lost Loved Ones

Dear Lord,

What would I do without you, especially when I am grieving the loss of a loved one? _____ was such an important part of my life. Now this person is gone. It feels as if a part of me has died, too.

I am so thankful to you, Lord, for walking with (and sometimes carrying) me through this valley. You treasure my tears, for they touch your heart. You hold me close through the dark times. You are there for me.

Thank you that death is not the end. If my loved ones knew you, I will see them again someday. You have made a way for us to enter heaven, where there will be no more tears or pain. It will be perfect, a place of peace. Thank you for providing your salvation to us.

Lord, I pray for those as they mourn the loss of their loved ones. Renew their peace, and comfort them in the way that only you can. Encircle them with whispers of love and encouragement. Tell them you are there and that you still have purposes and plans for them. You promise that, though sorrow lasts for the night, joy comes in the morning.

In Jesus' name I pray, amen.

"Don't be afraid, for I am with you. Don't be discouraged, for I am your God. I will strengthen you and help you. I will hold you up with my victorious right hand"
(Isa. 41:10).

Journal Your Thoughts

Day 165

Prayer for Those Who Have Experienced Trauma

Dear Lord,

Every individual is precious to you. It is impossible to fully grasp some of the horrific events that have happened in their lives. The truth is, many have been hurt by the ones they have trusted. The scars that form inside their souls are evident as they live out their lives trying to forget, but they can't.

Lord, I pray for those who suffered trauma as a child and still suffer from it today. Heal the wounds, not so that they forget what happened, but so that they can live lives that honor you. Give them healing and strength so that they may serve you and walk alongside others who have suffered as they have. Give them peace and security, knowing that you are with them and will never leave them. Show them, dear Lord, that you love them so much and are heartbroken over what happened to them. You care for us so much.

Everyone experiences the brokenness and pain of life, but you make sure that it doesn't go to waste. You bring beauty out of ashes. I pray that I would be able to join you in the healing process by offering myself as your hands and feet to help others feel your love. Help me to perceive their individual needs and guide me to care for them as you would.

In Jesus' name, amen.

"God is our refuge and strength, always ready to help in times of trouble" (Psalm 46:1).

Journal Your Thoughts

Day 166

Prayer for the Sexually Abused

Dear Compassionate Lord,

You created marriage and the sexual union between husband and wife. It was intended to be a beautiful reflection of your relationship with the Church, but flawed and sinful human beings have corrupted what you intended for good and have used it for evil.

Both men and women have misused this gift, and sex has been used to manipulate and cause pain. In some cases, it has been used as a tool of violence. It breaks your heart, Lord, and you weep with those who have been victims of rape, incest, and every form of sexual abuse and assault.

Lord, I pray for those who have been sexually abused. I pray that they would feel your healing touch. I pray that you would guide them in getting the help they need, whether it is through a counselor, a pastor, or a good friend. If they need to seek safety, Lord, guide them to the right place of protection and support. If they need to report abuse to the police, give them the courage to do so.

I also pray for those who have committed sexual abuse. Open their eyes to the pain they have caused. Create in them a new heart, and help them to repent of the evil they have done.

In the name of Jesus, I pray.

"Though you have made me see troubles, many and bitter, you will restore my life again; from the depths of the earth you will again bring me up" (Psalm 71:20).

Journal Your Thoughts

Day 167

Prayer for Those
Who Are Hungry

Dear Abba, Father,

So few of us know what it's like to be truly hungry. Yet there are millions of precious souls all over the world whose stomachs know the pain of hunger. Not hunger from being too busy to eat lunch, but the kind of gnawing emptiness from not having enough to eat for days, weeks, months, or even years.

I cannot imagine that kind of hunger, Lord, yet people right here where I live experience it every day. Comfort them. Help them to know that they are not forgotten. Send people to provide for their needs.

I ask you to provide for them, Lord. Not so they can have food, but to address the underlying issues that are causing them to go hungry in the first place. If they need a job, provide them with a job. If crops cannot grow because they are in an area experiencing drought, send rain. If they are in an abusive situation, lead them out. You know each person's situation, and I ask that you send the type of help they need to restore their health.

Thank you that your arm is not too short to reach anyone who is hungry. If you would have me play a role, whether that is taking someone a meal, donating to a charity, or directing people to the right government agencies so they can get the help they need, open my eyes and give me willing hands and feet to love them in your name.

In Jesus' name I pray, amen.

"Suppose you see a brother or sister who has no food or clothing, and you say, 'Good-bye and have a good day; stay

warm and eat well'—but then you don't give that person any food or clothing. What good does that do? So you see, faith by itself isn't enough. Unless it produces good deeds, it is dead and useless" (James 2:15–17).

Journal Your Thoughts

Day 168

Prayer for Natural Disasters

Dear Protector God,

Never do we feel more helpless than when a natural disaster strikes. Whether it's a tornado, earthquake, flood, or global crisis, we are faced with how limited our control really is.

We can build stronger buildings and reinforce retaining walls, but we cannot calm the earth or sea. We can wear protective masks and expand our hospital ICU capacity, but we cannot stop a new virus from emerging or create a vaccine in time to stop the global spread. Our inability to control such powerful forces terrifies us.

Yet none of these things takes you by surprise, God. The perfect plan you have for each one of our lives somehow anticipates and accommodates even the worst disasters. How wonderful you are that nothing—not toppled buildings, flooded cities, or crowded ICUs—can stop your plan and your love for us.

When disaster strikes, give us wisdom, God. Give us insight into the steps we should take to protect ourselves, our families, and our communities. But also give us peace that, when things are beyond our control, we can trust you. Even should we lose everything, we still have everything because our hope is not in the things of this world. Our hope is in how you use even the most difficult circumstances to grow us, shape us, and ultimately bless us by drawing us closer to you. Thank you that our home is in heaven, where there is no more pain, sorrow, or tears.

In your precious name, amen.

"He will wipe every tear from their eyes, and there will be no more death or sorrow or crying or pain. All these things are gone forever" (Rev. 21:4).

Journal Your Thoughts

Day 169

Prayer for Dealing with the Past

Dear Lord,

Pain from the past is not good to carry around. It is destructive. I, myself, have held on to things from my past to such an extent that it began eating away at me like a slow growing cancer. For years, I questioned, "Will the pain ever go away?" I wanted to forget, but life experiences kept triggering painful memories. Every time one of those memories was triggered, I hurt all over again.

Thank you for your wisdom in helping me through the pain. I pray for continued wisdom regarding what I need to bring to you to be healed from my past. You do not want me to be burdened by bitterness, anger, or disillusionment. You want me to be free to serve you always with a joyful heart and to love others.

I pray for those who still struggle with their pasts. The ghosts of painful events reappear over and over, and they can't seem to get rid of them. As they bring their hurts to you, I pray for your healing hand. I pray that you would give them complete healing so they would no longer be controlled by the past, but rather use their experiences as a testimony of your love and faithfulness. I pray that they would follow your leading in that journey of healing.

Jesus, there is a past, present, and future. Thank you that my past is not who I am. Thank you that my future looks bright because of you. I have victory over sin because of you. My past no longer has a hold on me, so I can dance with you in joyful freedom. Whether or not I dance, however, is my choice. I choose to dance.

In your precious name I pray, amen.

"Then Jesus said, 'Come to me, all of you who are weary and carry heavy burdens, and I will give you rest. Take my

yoke upon you. Let me teach you, because I am humble and gentle at heart, and you will find rest for your souls. For my yoke is easy to bear, and the burden I give you is light'" (Matt. 11:28–30).

Journal Your Thoughts

Day 170

Prayer for Emotional Freedom

Heavenly Father,

Thank you for the emotional freedom that you give me. Freedom is mine if I choose it. In following you, I can experience true freedom.

There are so many emotional prisons into which I put myself, and I need to break free. Jesus, you are the key to my cell. Please take my hand and lead me out so that I can have the abundant life you have planned. You have so much for me, and I don't want to miss any of it because I've locked myself away emotionally. I want to grow into the person you have meant for me to be.

Lord, I lift up to you those who are not experiencing emotional freedom and don't know how to find it. They are bound by worldly temptations and fears. I ask in your powerful name that you free them from these chains. Surround them with your grace and love so that they can experience your peace. They are highly valued by you. Help them put on the armor of God to protect themselves from binding spirits. I pray that they would grow more in freedom each day.

In your precious name I pray, amen.

"A final word: Be strong in the Lord and in his mighty power. Put on all of God's armor so that you will be able to stand firm against all strategies of the devil. For we are not fighting against flesh-and-blood enemies, but against evil rulers and authorities of the unseen world, against mighty powers in this dark world, and against evil spirits in the heavenly places" (Eph. 6:10–12).

Journal Your Thoughts

Day 171

Prayer for Discernment

Dear Heavenly Father,

I want to do the right thing. It is your wisdom that I desire in order to take the right steps through life. You know the path I should take, but how do I find it? How do I receive that insight?

The answers are in your Word. All the truth I need is there. If I want to see through your eyes and know what is on your heart, I need to steep myself in the Scriptures. I need to treasure verses in my heart by memorizing and living them. Each verse saturated in me will change me. To be wise, I must allow that to happen.

Lord, I pray for those who are seeking help, but don't look to you for it. They are relying on their own strength. Their strength is limited, but yours is not. I pray that they would be enlightened to that truth. Surround them with your presence, Lord, and whisper in their ears the great love you have for them. Draw them into the beauty of your truth.

In your precious and holy name, I pray, amen.

"If you need wisdom, ask our generous God, and he will give it to you. He will not rebuke you for asking" (James 1:5).

Journal Your Thoughts

Day 172

Prayer for Gaining Perspective

Dear Lord,

You have created me to have a mind . . . and to think. I pray that your wisdom would influence my view of the world. My perspective is a reflection of what I believe about you. If I am looking through the lens of your great love, I, too, will greatly love. I pray that I would not look through the lens of the world, which is tainted.

I lift up those to you who have a perspective that keeps them from living in joy and freedom. Their view on life and other people is so twisted that it keeps them from the positive emotions and perspectives that you want them to have. They find it difficult to love people. Instead, they feel threatened by them. I pray, Lord, that you would touch their hearts so that they would care about others the way you do. As they give themselves to others, loving them without condition, their joy and contentment will rise.

Lord, I pray that I would have your perspective on all things. I know you see it all—nothing is hidden from you. I can trust that the way you see things is the right way. I ask you to empower me to live what I believe. Loving God and loving people is the perspective you have called me to have and how you want me to live.

In Jesus' name I pray, amen.

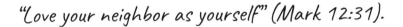

"Love your neighbor as yourself" (Mark 12:31).

Journal Your Thoughts

Day 173

Prayer for Having a Generous Spirit

Dear Lord,

Thank you for the generosity you have shown me. It always feels as if it is more than I deserve, but you bless me with great abundance anyway. I pray that I would be able to reflect your giving spirit with everyone. Nudge my heart, Jesus, when I need to give more. Help me not to hold back anything that you want me to give.

You own everything anyway. I am only a steward of all that you have given me. It is my job to take those blessings and use them to love and serve others.

I pray for those who have a difficult time sharing what they own. They fear that they will end up penniless, but Lord, you have a perfect plan for them. They can trust you with everything. You will provide for them. You own the cattle on a thousand hills. Your arm is not too short. Thank you for these promises in the Bible.

I pray that my generosity would stretch beyond finances and into other areas such as hospitality, volunteering, and gifts of time. May I hear you clearly when I am to have a generous heart and give without fear. I pray that you would be seen through my giving.

In Jesus' name I pray, amen.

"For all the animals of the forest are mine, and I own the cattle on a thousand hills. I know every bird on the mountains, and all the animals of the field are mine"
(Psalm 50:10-11).

Journal Your Thoughts

Day 174

Prayer for Releasing Control

Dear Lord,

I admit it—I want control. I want to hang on to my circumstances with my fists clenched tightly. Your Word says that you can drive better than I can, yet it is so hard to give up the steering wheel of my life.

Life can seem like a maze of city streets where I get lost and fearful. Yet what would happen if I trusted you completely? Lord, help me let go and allow you to take the wheel. At times, situations are out of my control. But you go before me. You lead me through, and you promise no harm will come to me.

I lift up those who are also trying to control their circumstances. Lord, you want to help them, but sometimes you wait until they are ready. When they get to the end of themselves—when they are finally willing to give up control—you will be there to pick them up and guide them. You will not wrestle control out of their hands. You are a patient God who will wait until they are ready.

Letting go is a process in which we learn to trust you more. It is part of our healing from the hurts of the world. Thank you, Lord.

In your name I pray, amen.

"Look here, you who say, 'Today or tomorrow we are going to a certain town and will stay there a year. We will do business there and make a profit.' How do you know what your life will be like tomorrow? Your life is like the morning fog—it's here a little while, then it's gone. What you ought to say is, 'If the Lord wants us to, we will live and do this or that'" (James 4:13–15).

Journal Your Thoughts

Day 175

Prayer for Being a
Good Role Model

Dear Father,

Having good role models in my life has made a huge difference, and I believe that you set that up for me. Thank you! These special people have shown me what is important in life. Their wisdom has impacted the choices I have made as I have grown older.

You gave us Jesus as the perfect role model. His life on earth made an impact for the world. He showed us what was important and gave us a better way to live. Your timing was perfect for this.

I pray in to being a good role model, too, and pray that others can also model for me at every age. I pray for those who need someone to help them turn their lives around. The models they are seeing on the streets and at home are not healthy. Bring people into their lives, dear Jesus, who can show them how you lived and help them see that better choices do pay off. Please protect them if they make the wrong choices. Your plan for them is great, Lord. I thank you ahead of time for the work you will be doing in their lives. May their lives be models of your glory.

In Jesus' name I pray, amen.

"Oh, the joys of those who do not follow the advice of the wicked, or stand around with sinners, or join in with mockers. But they delight in the law of the Lord, meditating on it day and night. They are like trees planted along the riverbank, bearing fruit each season. Their

leaves never wither, and they prosper in all they do"
(Psalm 1:1–3).

Journal Your Thoughts

Day 176

Prayer for Standing Firm on the Truth

Dear Lord,

I treasure all the truth that you have taught me over the years. Putting that truth into action is a challenge, especially when circumstances tempt me to turn from that truth. I become weak and find myself on a slippery slope. I want to stand firm on what I believe about you. I pray for the courage and strength to do this.

I desire for my character to be unyielding to the pressures of the world. In standing firm for you, Lord, I believe that my integrity is at its utmost. My ability to stand firm comes from you and is for your glory alone.

I pray for those who are wavering in their faith. Struggles are pulling them in different directions, and they can't seem to find solid ground on which to stand. I pray that they would pick up your Word and find encouragement to focus on you alone. May your Word, sharper than any double-edged sword, cut through the clutter in their minds and the lies they believe so they can see clearly to the root of the problem. Once the problem is clear, they will be able to discern the right path to take. I pray that they would be strong witnesses for you, Jesus.

I pray all this in your precious name, amen.

"Anyone who listens to my teaching and follows it is wise, like a person who builds a house on solid rock. Though the rain comes in torrents and the floodwaters rise and the winds beat against that house, it won't collapse because it is built on bedrock" (Matt. 7:24–25).

Journal Your Thoughts

Day 177

Prayer for Loving My Enemies

Dear Lord,

The pain that I have experienced at the hands of others is great. If I let it, this pain will be a source of growing bitterness. However, holding on to the hurt only allows me to be hurt repeatedly. Because of your great love for me, Jesus, I can let go of anger and free my soul to love my enemies. You have forgiven me for all I have done. I also need to let forgiveness flow freely from me to others. That is how I can love my enemies; the same way Jesus loves me.

I pray for anyone who is holding on to hate of their enemies. Lord, I pray that you would soften their hearts to see that there is a better way. Whatever the offense may have been, they can trust you to handle it. You see the big picture. The deepest, darkest secrets can be seen by you alone. You know why people act in certain ways. You are never surprised. None of us is totally good nor bad. You love us equally.

Today, I want to show love to my enemies. I want to reach out to them in your name and show them your love, who you are, and what you mean to me. It will always be for your glory, Lord.

In your precious name I pray, amen.

"You have heard the law that says, 'Love your neighbor' and hate your enemy. But I say, love your enemies! Pray for those who persecute you! In that way, you will be acting as true children of your Father in heaven. For he gives his sunlight to both the evil and the good, and he sends rain on the just and the unjust alike. If you love only those who love you, what reward is there for that?

Even corrupt tax collectors do that much. If you are kind only to your friends, how are you different from anyone else? Even pagans do that" (Matt. 5:43–47).

Journal Your Thoughts

Day 178

Prayer for Keeping Promises

Dear Lord,

I pray that when I make a promise, I would keep it. As flawed human beings, we have all failed to do this, myself included. It's so easy to make excuses, yet through Jesus, I know that I can keep my word just as you do.

Thank you for always keeping your promises. You never fail. There is nothing that will sway you from fulfilling your word. Great is your faithfulness. While the world holds on to promises loosely, you hold on to them tightly. I want to grasp the importance of my words and follow through on what I say. It is to your honor that I do this.

I pray for those who have not been able to do what they promise. They cannot be counted on, and I know that you want better for them. I pray that you would send good role models to them to show them how to keep their word. Help them understand the importance of this. Draw them close to you, Lord.

As words of promise spill from my lips, may my heart and mind be set on fulfilling them to your glory. I pray that I would never let the world draw me away from that.

In Jesus' name I pray, amen.

"A man who makes a vow to the Lord or makes a pledge under oath must never break it. He must do exactly what he said he would do" (Num. 30:2).

Journal Your Thoughts

Day 179

Prayer for Meaning What I Say

Dear Father,

The world is full of glib expressions that really mean nothing. We use words without thinking. I am guilty of doing this, as well. Forgive me, Jesus, for using words that are empty, reflecting my coldness of spirit towards the person to whom I am speaking. I desire to mean what I say. You always meant every word you said. Your Word is a treasure.

Lord, help me to remember that each person I come in contact with is a precious treasure to you. When I say I will pray for them, it is my responsibility to follow through. If I ask how they are doing, I should really want to know.

I pray for those who don't seem to be able to focus outside themselves and fulfill what they say they will do. They have many tasks to complete. Their priorities overshadow the compassion and mercy they need to relate to others. I pray that their priorities would change as their hearts are changed. You are the holder of their hearts. Open their eyes to see the importance of following through for others. May their heart break for what breaks yours. I pray that they would respond accordingly and mean it.

In Jesus' name I pray, amen.

"Just say a simple, 'Yes, I will' or 'No, I won't.' Anything beyond this is from the evil one" (Matt. 5:37).

Journal Your Thoughts

Day 180

Prayer Against Our Expectations

Dear Jesus,

The way I think life should go is often very different from how you see it. I pray for eyes to see and ears to hear. Whenever I set up an expectation for someone or something, I set myself up for disappointment. I pray against creating expectations that are not of you. Forgive me for the many times that I have done this.

I pray for those who want to control others through their expectations. It isn't right to treat others in this manner, so help them to see that. We cannot enforce our expectations on others. This takes away their freedom and damages relationships.

I also pray for all those towards whom I have ungodly expectations. Help me break that sinful cycle and allow your children to grow according to your expectations, not mine. Give me the opportunity to ask for their forgiveness in the near future.

Help me to release the expectations I have on myself. Having these expectations causes me to feel unworthy when I don't meet them. In your eyes, I *am* worthy. Thank you, Jesus! You set the standard for who I am and who I should be. Because of your love, grace, and mercy, I am accepted.

In your name I pray, amen.

"Yes, each of us will give a personal account to God. So let's stop condemning each other. Decide instead to live in such a way that you will not cause another believer to stumble and fall" (Rom. 14:12–13).

Journal Your Thoughts

Day 181

Prayer Against Comparing Myself to Others

Dear Lord,

I look in the mirror and find fault. It's because I compare myself with others. I pray that I don't hold others as the model, but only you, Jesus. As I study your Word, I pray that I would learn how I should live. The standard on this earth is not high, and I pray that I would not reach for that standard, but yours.

I pray for those who feel unacceptable because their friends all wear the same brand-name clothes, live in big houses, or drive sporty cars. I pray against the desire to play the comparison game. Lord, I know you created them perfectly and that your plan for them is good. I pray they would find encouragement from people that you send to them. Those who focus on seeking you rather than the world are fountains of encouragement. I pray they would splash it on each other.

I pray against the poisoning of my mind by the media, which tries to set the standard of how we should live and be. These lies affect so many young minds, and I pray that the truth of who they are would come forth and drown out the world's faulty thinking.

In Jesus' precious name I pray, amen.

"Obviously, I'm not trying to win the approval of people, but of God. If pleasing people were my goal, I would not be Christ's servant" (Gal. 1:10).

Journal Your Thoughts

Day 182

Prayer Against Envy

Dear Heavenly Father,

You are the giver of every good thing, and you have taken care of me for many years. I praise and thank you for the goodness shown to me. I pray that I would be grateful for everything. Envy is sin. That is how sin came into the Garden of Eden. Adam and Eve were envious of you. They wanted to be like you, so they bit into the fruit, and the demon of envy slithered in. I pray that the snake would be kept from me. I do not want to carry envy anywhere in my heart.

I pray for those who are struggling with envy right now. I pray that they would experience freedom by choosing to follow your ways. May any indication of wanting something or someone else be a trigger for them to realign with your way. I pray that they would know that what you provide is sufficient.

Grant me a spirit, Lord, that is always thankful to you. There is nothing in this world I need more than you, and I have that. Praise Jesus that this truth lives in me. Help me, Lord, to share that truth with others so that they can see where they are now is perfect in your sight. May they see the blessings that surround them.

In Jesus' name I pray, amen.

"A peaceful heart leads to a healthy body; jealousy is like cancer in the bones" (Prov. 14:30).

Journal Your Thoughts

Day 183

Prayer Against Materialism

Dear Father God,

I look around and see all of the things that I have accumulated. Many of these things I have not touched for years. How did I get so much stuff? I would feel as if I needed something, buy it, and then forget about it or go on to the next thing. It is an endless cycle. I pray that I would end that cycle today. I don't want to thirst for material things. I want to thirst for only you, dear Lord. You are all that really matters. I will be with you for eternity, while the stuff around me will dissolve.

I pray for those who are constantly purchasing clothing, jewelry, or big-ticket items. What hole in their lives are they trying to fill? It is an empty exercise. If you are not at the center of their choices, then those choices are worthless. I pray that their hearts would be filled with you. That kind of satisfaction will last forever.

Lord, if you have a purpose for an item in my life, then I will praise you with it. The blessings given to me I will use to bless another. Help me to take nothing for granted. I will be content with what you give me and praise you for it.

In Jesus' name I pray, amen.

"Yet true godliness with contentment is itself great wealth. After all, we brought nothing with us when we came into the world, and we can't take anything with us when we leave it. So if we have enough food and clothing, let us be content" (1 Tim. 6:6–8).

Journal Your Thoughts

Day 184

Prayer for Going the Extra Mile

Dear Lord,

You do not desire for any of us to work beyond what we are able. Your plan is perfect. Yet, sometimes you give us more energy to go beyond what is expected or even what seems humanly possible. People are often surprised when others go beyond their expectations. We do this in order to give you the glory so that others can see your greatness. I love serving you, and time spent helping others is never wasted. You will use it.

I pray for those who get frustrated when they go beyond their comfort zones and are not recognized for it. I pray that you would send peace to their hearts. Help them realize that it is not about them, but you. You recognize every offering they make. You are the only audience that matters.

I ask that my heart and mind be transformed so that I would always want to go the extra mile for others. May I be attentive to how I can do more for someone and bless them abundantly as you have blessed me. Nudge me in that direction, Jesus. Let my actions touch the hearts of others so that they would be drawn closer to you. I pray that you would enlarge my territory and grant me opportunities to bless others in your name. Thank you!

In Jesus' precious name I pray, amen.

"If a soldier demands that you carry his gear for a mile, carry it two miles" (Matt. 5:41).

Journal Your Thoughts

Day 185

Prayer When I Need to Confront Someone in Love

Dear Lord,

Relationships can be difficult, especially when the other person does something that goes against your Word. We may know that you are calling us to confront them, but how? Confrontation can be uncomfortable and even difficult.

I acknowledge that I don't like conflict. It has never been my desire to bring open confrontation, so when that becomes necessary, give me the courage to confront and say what needs to be said in love. I pray that I would have love for each person just as you do. If someone needs to be confronted, help my words not to come from a place of hurt but from a desire to understand.

For those who have a hard time with confrontation as I do, give them the strength and peace to confront as needed. For those who are bold in confrontation, give them grace so that the interaction would be gentle and not harsh or in a spirit of condemnation. I pray for reconciliation in relationships. May those who are confronted not feel resentful, but have ears to hear.

I pray for the same attitude when I am confronted by someone. May I be willing, not just to listen, but to truly hear what they have to say. Help me to desire healing in the relationship more than I want to defend myself. I believe that is what you desire, too. When I am confronted, may I be humble.

In your name I pray, amen.

"A servant of the Lord must not quarrel but must be kind to everyone, be able to teach, and be patient with difficult people. Gently instruct those who oppose the truth.

Perhaps God will change those people's hearts, and they will learn the truth" (2 Tim. 2:24–25).

Journal Your Thoughts

Day 186

Prayer for Confidence

Dear Precious Lord,

Sometimes I shy away from opportunities because my confidence is low. Help me to seek you for encouragement and allow you to energize my passion. I believe that you can do anything. There is no reason for me to doubt when you call me to do something. My confidence is in you. I pray that truth would give me the strength to go forward.

I pray for others who need a confidence boost, too. I pray that you would show them that they can do it. You will walk with them and help them. I pray that they would allow you to enable them, equip them, and work through them for any task you set before them. In trusting you, they will be blessed.

I pray that my confidence would not turn into ego. Ego can be destructive, both with others and with you. I want to focus only on serving you. When it becomes more than that, I become double-minded. I can be confident because I am yours. You created me to do good works, and it is my choice to do that for you today and every day. I have confidence that you will empower me to do great things, for it is promised in your Word. It is truly for your glory.

In Jesus' name I pray, amen.

"Now to him who is able to do far more abundantly than all that we ask or think, according to the power at work within us" (Eph. 3:20).

Journal Your Thoughts

Day 187

Prayer Against Fear

Dear Jesus,

I admit that sometimes I am afraid. I know that you hold all things in your hands, but in my weakness, I fear. Sometimes I am afraid of things I know, and sometimes I am afraid of things I imagine. Either way, I am afraid.

Thank you, Jesus, that you are my strong tower. Every time I fear, I pray that I would run into your tower of protection and strength so that I can have the same courage as King David. You surround me with protection—that is truth. You send your angels to help me. I pray that my heart and mind can stand on that truth.

I pray for those who don't feel safe. I pray for your protection as they go through this struggle. I pray for a peaceful outcome. You hold them in your hand, Lord, and I pray that the choices they make will be glorifying to you. I pray that they would discern right from wrong and keep safe. There are consequences for choices that do not please you.

Lord, I ask for protection as I take each step through my days. I want to serve you, and pray for a shield around me so that I can fulfill your plans for my life. I command Satan's darts to bounce off me! I think of the angels on steeds that surrounded your prophets in the Old Testament. I believe that it is true for me today.

In Jesus' name I pray, amen.

"Those who live in the shelter of the Most High will find rest in the shadow of the Almighty. This I declare about the Lord: He alone is my refuge, my place of safety; he is my God, and I trust him. For he will rescue you from every trap and protect you from deadly disease. He will cover you

with his feathers. He will shelter you with his wings. His faithful promises are your armor and protection. Do not be afraid of the terrors of the night, nor the arrow that flies in the day. Do not dread the disease that stalks in darkness, nor the disaster that strikes at midday" (Psalm 91:1-6).

Journal Your Thoughts

_____

_____

_____

_____

_____

_____

_____

_____

_____

_____

_____

_____

_____

_____

_____

_____

_____

_____

Day 188

Prayer to Stand Through Spiritual Warfare

Dear Lord,

"The battle belongs to the Lord." I have heard that said many times, but do I truly believe it? You are the Almighty, and no one can beat you in any battle. I pray that I would be as confident in this truth as King David when he stood up to Goliath. I pray for this confidence both physically and spiritually. King David had victory because of you. His confidence stood through all of his challenges in life. I want to stand on that same firm foundation. Help me do this, Jesus. It is through your strength that I can achieve this.

I pray for all who are fighting battles in their own strength. Lord, I pray that they would look to you for their victory. Remind them to clothe themselves in the spiritual armor you have prepared for them. It is already there — they simply need to receive it. The world wants to deceive them into believing they have lost the battle, but that is a lie. Your light can bring them out to the truth. Shine brightly, Jesus!

Spiritual warfare is always needed. I pray that I would put on the armor you have given me and confidently go forth into battle, confident of victory. I pray that I would not waiver. Help me grip the Sword of Truth tightly and wield it with confidence.

In Jesus' name I pray, amen.

"Be strong in the Lord and in his mighty power. Put on all of God's armor so that you will be able to stand firm against all strategies of the devil. For we are not fighting against flesh-and-blood enemies, but against evil rulers and authorities of the unseen world, against mighty powers in this dark world, and against evil spirits in the heavenly places. Therefore, put on every piece of God's armor so you will be able to resist the enemy in the time of evil. Then after the battle you will still be standing firm. Stand your ground, putting on the belt of truth and the body armor of God's righteousness. For shoes, put on the peace that comes from the Good News so that you will be fully prepared. In addition to all of these, hold up the shield of faith to stop the fiery arrows of the devil. Put on salvation as your helmet, and take the sword of the Spirit, which is the word of God" (Eph. 6:10–17).

Journal Your Thoughts

Day 189

Prayer for Transformation

Dear Lord,

Give me a heart that is pure. Transformation by your hand will create in me the clean heart that I desire. The process of transformation includes ridding my heart of toxins. These are the sins that lay in wait to appear. I am tempted by these toxins to go against God. It is not what I want. Help me, Jesus, in doing what is right. Help me to throw away all the trash in my soul.

I pray specifically for those whose hearts are burdened with obstacles in their faith walk. They are tripping over temptations, and this is affecting the health of their hearts. These hearts are not beating in rhythm with your ways. I ask that you draw them to you and transform them into the people you meant for them to be. You love them and want them to experience all the blessings you have in store.

Transformation is spiritual surgery. It's painful, but the results can be gratifying. My goal is to reflect your Son in my daily living. I believe that I can do this in your power. You inspire me to make better choices. You love me totally even when I fail. You pick me up and brush me off, take my hand, and help me walk again. You transform my heart. Thank you!

In Jesus' name I pray, amen.

"Create in me a clean heart, O God. Renew a loyal spirit within me. Do not banish me from your presence, and don't take your Holy Spirit from me. Restore to me the joy of your salvation, and make me willing to obey you"
(Psalm 51:10–12).

Journal Your Thoughts

Day 190

Prayer for Running the Race

Dear Lord,

Each day gives me opportunity to serve you faithfully. You have set a race before me, so help me to continue on that run until I cross the finish line. So many times, I am tripped up by debris on the track. The world throws temptations, tragedies, and other challenges that cause me to stumble. Thank you for your faithfulness in getting me back up and helping me to stay focused on the goal.

I pray for those who are running a different race. They are running after things of the world and believe they will find their peace and contentment in them. They think that having the right job, a beautiful home, children, and other earthly things that meet the expectations placed on them by society are what they need to be successful. Jesus, you modeled a different way.

You never meant for me or anyone else to run alone, and we are *not* alone. Even when we do not have earthly things, you are still with us. We can also be there for each other. Sometimes I fall on the track. It is good to know that others are there to pick me up and help me finish the race. Use me to do the same for others.

In Jesus' name I pray, amen.

"Don't you realize that in a race everyone runs, but only one person gets the prize? So run to win! All athletes are disciplined in their training. They do it to win a prize that will fade away, but we do it for an eternal prize. So I run with purpose in every step. I am not just shadowboxing. I discipline my body like an athlete, training it to do what it

should. Otherwise, I fear that after preaching to others I myself might be disqualified" (1 Cor. 9:24-27).

Journal Your Thoughts

_____

_____

_____

_____

_____

_____

_____

_____

_____

_____

_____

_____

_____

_____

_____

_____

_____

_____

_____

_____

_____

Day 191

Prayer Against Being Consumed with Busyness

Dear Heavenly Father,

Busyness can be an addiction for many of us, and it can sap our energy so that our lives feel out of control. Lord, I pray for those who are experiencing this type of busyness. I ask you to show them how to better manage their time, and where to invest their time, so that they can see that there is a better way to live that is fulfilling and restoring. I pray that they would obey and follow that plan.

May their eyes be open to the blessings you have given them. Help them to see that everything they value—their family, work, friends, their homes—are gifts from you. They have these things, not through their busyness, but by your gracious hand. I pray that their lives would be enriched as they rediscover the gift of your grace.

I pray for those I know who want to meet the needs of everyone around them. They are wearing themselves out trying to take on responsibilities that are not theirs to take. I pray for balance to be brought into their lives. The time they spend at your feet is far more important than the time they are out being "busy."

I pray for people who feel they are valued by what they do rather than who they are and *whose* they are. They are yours, dear Lord. That alone gives them high value. May they experience your peace in realizing that truth.

I pray this in Jesus' name, amen.

"Whatever is good and perfect is a gift coming down to us from God our Father, who created all the lights in the

heavens. He never changes or casts a shifting shadow"
(James 1:17).

Journal Your Thoughts

Day 192

Prayer for Rest

Dear Father,

As any new mother knows, rest is a beautiful thing. I pray for the tired souls who fight just to get through every day. They pour so much into others. They try to please everyone, but that is an impossible task. Jesus, I pray for them to have rest. I pray that they would allow themselves to rest in your presence and become refreshed in your Spirit.

Lord, I particularly pray for those who are beyond tired. They rush around at work, then rush home where new responsibilities await them. The only time they really seem to have to themselves is when they collapse into bed. Lord, there is so much more that you have planned for them.

Sometimes, we need to hang on and fight through the exhaustion. Other times, we need to let go of things to which we are clinging tightly, but which we really need to release to you. Help us discern which is which.

You have given us a day of rest, Jesus, and sometimes we use it as just another day to get things done rather than what it was meant to be, a day of rejuvenation. Spending time with you and family refreshes us so that we can face the next day, the next week, and the months ahead. Help us intentionally use our day of rest so that we may be strong for you.

In Jesus' name I pray, amen.

"It is useless for you to work so hard from early morning until late at night, anxiously working for food to eat; for God gives rest to his loved ones" (Psalm 127:2).

Journal Your Thoughts

Day 193

Prayer for Energy

Dear Father,

Every day, there are so many demands on my time and energy. I try to get everything done, but I fall short and never seem to have enough energy to do it all well. I'm tired. When I get home from working all day, there's little energy left. Show me, Jesus, how to use my time wisely.

I also pray for those who feel as if they are dragging. Lord, I pray for your Spirit to come afresh on them. Your Spirit can energize anyone. I ask that they would surrender to you whatever is weighing them down. Lighten their loads, Lord, so that they can freely lift up their hands in praise to you.

I also pray for energy in my spirit. I want to be energized by you so that my faith is glowing for all to see. I want to be inspired to go forth with passion, I want to go where you want me to go and do what you want me to do. With you, I can step out of the boat and walk on water. It is all for your glory, Lord!

In Jesus' name I pray, amen.

"So be careful how you live. Don't live like fools, but like those who are wise. Make the most of every opportunity in these evil days. Don't act thoughtlessly, but understand what the Lord wants you to do" (Eph. 5:15–17).

Journal Your Thoughts

Day 194

Prayer for Rain

Dear Lord,

I pray for the lands that are experiencing lack of rain. Without rain, crops do not grow, communities do not eat, and husbands and fathers cannot provide for their families. The stress that comes with being unable to support loved ones is overwhelming, and I pray that you would show each and every person affected by drought that your hand is not too short to provide for them. Surround them with your people to help them make ends meet. Your people are blessed to be a blessing.

When rain comes down on the earth, it fulfills so many needs. Without rain, the land cannot be nourished. It becomes like a desert. Our souls are like that, Lord. Without the living water you provide, we become parched and dry in our spiritual walks. May your Spirit reign inside us for eternity.

I pray specifically for the areas where the people are struggling with drought and the earth is parched. The water table goes lower and lower, with no end in sight. Lord, they need a miracle from you. God, you can do this with a word, for all things are commanded by you.

In Jesus' name I pray, amen.

"Elijah was as human as we are, and yet when he prayed earnestly that no rain would fall, none fell for three and a half years! Then, when he prayed again, the sky sent down rain and the earth began to yield its crops"
(James 5:17–18).

Journal Your Thoughts

Day 195

Prayer for Mentors

Dear Jesus,

You know that mentors are special gifts to people. You equip them to be able to walk with others through their faith journeys to encourage and pray for them as well as be a model and friend. The heart of a mentor is giving. They give of themselves. Wisdom that comes from life experience is invaluable. They are blessed to be a blessing. Thank you for the mentors you have put in my life.

Use me, Lord, to be a mentor to others. I want to pass on the blessing to those with whom I come in contact each day. I believe, Jesus, that you have special people in my life to mentor. May I do it humbly and in honor of you.

I pray for those who need or want a mentor. Bring someone into their lives in ways that will uplift them. Right now, I have _____ in mind. If you want them to have a mentor, please make it clear whether you want that person to be me. If not, I pray that you would raise up a healthy mentoring relationship with another. Thank you for the greatest mentor of all, Jesus.

It is in his name I pray, amen.

"Plans go wrong for lack of advice; many advisers bring success" (Prov. 15:22).

Journal Your Thoughts

Day 196

Prayer for Sharing My Faith

Dear Lord,

You have walked with me many years, and I praise you for all the blessings I have experienced along the way. I pray that I would be willing to share my journey with others. Give me the opportunities and courage to share how you have worked in my life. The struggles and triumphs are many, and they were all put into place for your glory. You have given me a testimony to share. This is a gift that I am not to keep to myself. I pray for courage to tell of your wonderful works.

I pray for those who are nervous about sharing their faith. I pray that they would be able to see the benefits of telling others about you and not worry about what they will think. You are all that matters. You will give them the words to say; they just need to be open and willing to share those words.

I pray that I would be available for your use, as well. I want to share the greatness of your love. I want to help people connect with you so that their hurts can be healed. You alone are the Great Healer. Your love casts out the darkness from inside us and replaces it with light, joy, and peace. You are worthy of all praise.

In Jesus' name I pray, amen.

"I am certain that God, who began the good work within you, will continue his work until it is finally finished on the day when Christ Jesus returns" (Phil. 1:6).

Journal Your Thoughts

Day 197

Prayer for Missionaries

Dear Lord,

There are special people whom you have created with a passion for going outside their own boxes and ministering to others. For those who have this call, I pray that they would have every provision imaginable to fulfill it. You are the Great Provider and will not allow your mission to fail.

I pray for those who are called to be missionaries in another part of the world. Keep them safe, Lord. Help them build deep and meaningful relationships that will enable them to share the gospel with ears that are willing to hear. Give them good health as they are serving, clarity of mind in speaking for you, and a joy that exceeds all things. You are with them, and I pray that they would experience your presence as they show a hurting world the healing and powerful love of Jesus Christ.

Thank you, Lord, for the people you call to be missionaries afar, but also for those who answer the call to serve right here at home. That might be in the inner city, on a reservation, or in our own neighborhoods. Whoever we are and wherever we are called to serve, we have a responsibility to share about you. I pray that we would take this calling seriously. You give us opportunities to do this in obedience to you so that others may come to know you as Lord and Savior.

In Jesus' precious name I pray, amen.

"Therefore, go and make disciples of all the nations, baptizing them in the name of the Father and the Son and the Holy Spirit. Teach these new disciples to obey all the commands I have given you. And be sure of this: I am

with you always, even to the end of the age"
(Matt. 28:19–20).

Journal Your Thoughts

Day 198

Prayer for Those with Addictions

Dear Abba, Father,

I pray for people who want to escape the pain and trauma in their lives and think that their addiction is the answer. Whatever they are addicted to—drugs, sex, alcohol, shopping, gambling—may numb the pain for a little while, but you know that the problem is still there and will rise up again. When it does, that pain drives them deeper into addiction, and the cycle continues.

God, this is not the plan you have for them. You do not desire us to have pain and struggle, but when those things come, you use these struggles as opportunities for growth and for us to become stronger in our faith. Addiction blocks the work you are doing in our lives. I pray against all addictions and temptations that keep us from you.

I pray that people's eyes would be open to the fact that even their "little addictions" are blocking their path to freedom. Open their eyes, Lord. Help them turn from anything they are doing to numb their pain. I pray that they would receive the message that there is a better way and that your way is perfect.

I pray specifically for those who have allowed Satan to have footholds in their lives through their addictions. Your love for them is greater, and I trust you, God, that you will do what is needed to bring them to freedom in you. Surround them with your love so that they can shine for your glory in this life.

In Jesus' name I pray, amen.

"Stay alert! Watch out for your great enemy, the devil. He prowls around like a roaring lion, looking for someone to

devour. Stand firm against him, and be strong in your faith. Remember that your family of believers all over the world is going through the same kind of suffering you are. In his kindness God called you to share in his eternal glory by means of Christ Jesus. So after you have suffered a little while, he will restore, support, and strengthen you, and he will place you on a firm foundation. All power to him forever!" (1 Pet. 5:8–11).

Journal Your Thoughts

Day 199

Prayer for Alcoholics

Dear Lord,

The damage done by alcohol is huge; not only in the person's body, but also in their relationships, their finances, and their families. I pray that all of those struggling with alcoholism would find the strength from you to release the drink from their hands and turn to you for support instead.

Recovery from alcoholism is so difficult. Even those who successfully complete treatment still feel the pull for the rest of their lives. Staying sober takes constant vigilance and self-control. I pray for that power from your hand to steer them clear from drinking.

Families carry the scars of alcoholism, as well, and I pray for their healing, too. I also pray for other members of the alcoholic's family who suffer from the disease. I pray for protection over their minds and hearts that you may override any desire they may have to turn to alcohol as their loved one has done. You have a better plan for them.

The temptation to join in on unhealthy alcohol consumption is everywhere, and we must be strong to fight against it. I pray that more of your light would be shown on the devastation of alcoholism rather than the manipulated "fun times" manufactured by the media. The glorification of alcoholism is a lie. I pray that those addicted could break free from their chains as they sit at your feet to find a better way.

I pray these things in Jesus' name, amen.

"Don't be drunk with wine, because that will ruin your life. Instead, be filled with the Holy Spirit" (Eph. 5:18).

Journal Your Thoughts

Day 200

Prayer for Drug Users

Dear Jesus,

The substances used to ease the pain of life are many, but they are not effective. Even the strongest drug cannot heal us from the pain that is inside.

Drugs seem to be the answer at the beginning, but over time, people need more and more of these drugs to mask the pain. The result is a devastating cycle that draws them deeper into addiction. They lose their health, their jobs, and their loved ones. Sometimes, they even lose their lives.

You are the only way for us to be free from pain. True freedom only comes when we allow you to heal us from the inside. It is a difficult journey, but we do not walk it alone. You walk it with us. I pray that your light would shine in the lives of those who abuse drugs. Identifying the problem is the first step.

I pray for all those who struggle with using drugs. In many cases, they are already experiencing the consequences of drug abuse in their lives, even if they aren't willing or able to recognize it. Grab their hearts, Lord, and show them the truth. Give them the strength to turn around and walk away from the drug life.

I lift up all who are looking for a high, and that they find it in you, Lord Jesus. Your presence in the lives of your people makes it possible for us to experience your freedom and joy.

In your name I pray, amen.

"When you follow the desires of your sinful nature, the results are very clear: sexual immorality, impurity, lustful pleasures, idolatry, sorcery, hostility, quarreling, jealousy, outbursts of anger, selfish ambition, dissension, division, envy, drunkenness, wild parties, and other sins like these.

Let me tell you again, as I have before, that anyone living that sort of life will not inherit the Kingdom of God" (Gal. 5:19–21).

Journal Your Thoughts

Day 201

Prayer for Those Experiencing Chronic Pain

Heavenly Father,

Life can be hard, but when chronic physical pain is added into the mix, it is very difficult to function. Some days, we want to give up.

I pray for those who feel as if they are hanging on by a thread and slipping. Your Spirit, dear Jesus, can keep them holding on, for it is worth it. You have not left them, and you promise to lift them up with your righteous right hand.

I pray for those experiencing chronic pain every day. I want to reach out and help them. If you want to use me to bring help and support, I am willing. However, there might not be anything I can do to ease the pain. I pray for their doctors to be able to monitor what medications work for them. I pray for your healing touch that they may walk the rest of their journeys pain-free. You have so much planned for them, yet it's hard to see when the focus is on the pain. I pray that you would bring them relief.

Lord, help us all be sensitive to those who are suffering from chronic pain. We cannot judge what they are experiencing. The pain is theirs alone. Help us to bring them encouragement and perhaps distract them from the pain for a little while.

In Jesus' name I pray, amen.

"Wherever he went—in villages, cities, or the countryside—they brought the sick out to the marketplaces. They begged him to let the sick touch at least the fringe of his robe, and all who touched him were healed" (Mark 6:56).

Journal Your Thoughts

Day 202

Prayer for Emotional Pain

Dear Jesus,

I can't imagine some of the pain people are experiencing from their emotional wounds. Touch their hearts and souls so they can experience healing. Your truth can be a soothing balm. I pray that those who are hurting would be drawn to the reading of your Word so that they can experience your love and grace and see the power you have over all things. You have not abandoned them. You are in the midst of their pain and holding on to them tightly.

I lift up those whose emotional pain feels as if it is more than they can bear. The memories of what happened replay in their minds over and over again. I pray for their release from this prison. Break the chains that bind their minds so that they can live in total freedom. That's what you want for them—bring it on!

Emotional pain takes a toll on physical health, too, so I pray for healing for both the mind and body for those who suffer with deep emotional pain. Help them, Lord, to be completely healed in your name.

Amen.

"Why am I discouraged? Why is my heart so sad? I will put my hope in God! I will praise him again—my Savior and my God!" (Psalm 42:11).

Journal Your Thoughts

Day 203

Prayer for Those Who Feel Insecure

Dear Heavenly Father,

I pray for those who feel that the world is a dangerous place. They may feel powerless and weak, with no clear direction. That is a scary thing. I pray that you would fill them with hope. You have made us who follow you secure in our destinies, and not only that, but secure in your love and grace throughout each day. In your Word, you have told us repeatedly not to fear because we are in your hand at all times.

I pray for those who are afraid of many things and unsure of what they should do. I pray for those who are unsure of who they really are and what purpose they have in life. This insecurity causes much stress, and I ask for your intervention. I pray that they would see you as the strong foundation on which they can stand and that they would have no fear. Thank you, Lord, for your promise that you will always hold them up.

I pray that I would feel secure in you at all times, not just when things are going great. I pray, too, that I would encourage others to live the same lives of security.

I pray this in your name, amen.

"My sheep listen to my voice; I know them, and they follow me. I give them eternal life, and they will never perish. No one can snatch them away from me, for my Father has given them to me, and he is more powerful than anyone else. No one can snatch them from the Father's hand" (John 10:27–29).

Journal Your Thoughts

Day 204

Prayer for Those Who Need Hope

Dear Jesus,

I pray for people who struggle with hopelessness and lack the motivation to move on. They try to overcome their problems only to be knocked down again. Send others to come around them and help them stand. Send people to speak your words of encouragement for them to hear and believe. The hope you have for them is overflowing and will never run out.

I pray for those who feel as if life has let them down and there is nowhere for them to go. They desperately need your hope to survive each crisis that besets them, especially when these crises seem to have no end. I pray that your Holy Spirit would fill their hearts with courage as you speak to them. You are at work in them, Jesus, and I thank you for what you will do. It will glorify you, and your great work in their lives will give encouragement to others.

The arrival of hope in any life can transform it totally. I pray for that transformation in me and all others who call you Lord and Savior. Draw them to you, Lord, so that you can do a new work in them and bring a spirit of peace and joy.

I pray these things in your precious name, amen.

"I pray that God, the source of hope, will fill you completely with joy and peace because you trust in him. Then you will overflow with confident hope through the power of the Holy Spirit" (Rom. 15:13).

Journal Your Thoughts

Day 205

Prayer for Those Who Are Unable to Have Children

Dear Abba, Father,

I pray for those whose arms are empty of their own babies. For whatever reason, they have been unable to bear children. I pray for your comfort in their lives. Children are truly a blessing from you. I pray for the bitterness that can set in for young couples who have no children. I ask for their protection and that Satan would not be allowed to gain a foothold through discouragement.

You have created so many beautiful children, and I thank you for that. I pray that connections can be made through adoption agencies to have a child. Give the couples unable to have their own children a heart for adoption, dear Lord, just as you have adopted us into your family. There is so much love to be shared in these families. Thank you for supplying their every need.

I pray for the couples who have been trying for years unsuccessfully to adopt a child. I see their broken hearts whenever they are around children, and my heart aches for them. However, I know that your plan for them is perfect. I ask that you give them a heart of peace as they seek your will in their lives.

In Jesus' name I pray, amen.

"Not that I was ever in need, for I have learned how to be content with whatever I have. I know how to live on almost nothing or with everything. I have learned the secret of living in every situation, whether it is with a full stomach or empty, with plenty or little. For I can do

everything through Christ, who gives me strength"
(Phil. 4:11–13).

Journal Your Thoughts

Day 206

Prayer for Parents

Dear Father God,

Being a parent is the most difficult, yet rewarding job in the world. It is an honor to be chosen by you to be a parent. I pray that no one takes that role for granted. Raising a child is a tremendous responsibility, but you promise to help all parents as they raise their children in you. Thank you for your grace and mercy as they journey through parenthood.

Lord, I pray for those who are going through a tough time with their children, especially when those children are suffering from illness, trauma, or rebellion. When a child suffers, it is both exhausting and terrifying. For parents, sometimes it feels as if it is more than they can bear. I pray for your strength to uphold them to persevere.

Help parents remember that, while you have trusted them with their children on earth, ultimately, those children are being cared for by you. Your strength is greater than theirs. Your arm is never too short. You never grow tired or weary, and your strength will never fail. You will help them make it to the goal. Help these parents keep their eyes on you. The children you have given them are precious to you. You know each one by name, and you care about them.

I pray that parents would remember the power of prayer. Prayer can do so much more than words. Encourage them to model their prayer life in front of their children so that those children can see what a relationship with you looks like. Witnessing this lifestyle of prayer will also give a great testimony to children of how much they are loved and how much God loves them.

Help parents never to weary in lifting up their children on a daily basis, for this is what will keep them on the right track.

In Jesus' name I pray, amen.

"How joyful is the man whose quiver is full of them! He will not be put to shame when he confronts his accusers at the city gates" (Psalm 127:5).

Journal Your Thoughts

_____

_____

_____

_____

_____

_____

_____

_____

_____

_____

_____

_____

_____

_____

_____

_____

_____

_____

_____

_____

_____

Day 207

Prayer for Adoptive and Blended Families

Dear Abba, Father.

There are so many different kinds of families, and sometimes those families include adoptive or stepparents. Parents who are raising non-biological children have all the challenges of biological parents, plus the added challenges that come with blending two families into one.

Sometimes adoptive and stepparents accept these children as their own. You would never know, by looking at the relationship, that these children were not from their own bodies. There is love and trust between both parent and child. Thank you, Lord, for the blessing of blended families like these.

In other families, children do not always feel accepted. They feel different from their parents' biological children. They feel "less than." Some even suffer abuse and neglect. God, your heart breaks for these children. You see them, and you are with them. Help them to see that any lack of acceptance from a step- or adoptive parent is not from you. I pray that they would not associate any lack of love or acceptance from these parents as reflecting the love and trust they have in you.

Help blended and adoptive families come together as one. Where there is suspicion, hurt, or lack of love, bring healing. Restore broken relationships and grow the love and trust these children deserve. Blended and adoptive parents have a special role and special responsibility. Help them carry it out well, and help their relationship with their children truly reflect your love.

In Jesus' name, I pray, amen.

"I pray that they will all be one, just as you and I are one—as you are in me, Father, and I am in you. And may

they be in us so that the world will believe you sent me"
(John 17:21).

Journal Your Thoughts

Day 208

Prayer for Single Parents

Dear Abba, Father,

You are the perfect father. You know how difficult parenting is. It is difficult, God, even when there are two parents in the home. It is that much more difficult when there is only one.

A single parent is their child's primary teacher, role model, and caregiver. This can be exhausting, Lord. A single parent carries all of these responsibilities alone. When it comes to shopping, meal preparation, and housework, there is no one else to help. In the middle of the night, no matter how tired, stressed, or sick a single parent might be, they are on call. It is on them to pick the kids up from the bus stop, help with homework, and transport children everywhere they need to go. Single parents rarely get a break.

Give single parents extra strength and endurance, Lord. Help them to draw on your strength when they need to wake up multiple times a night to change a diaper, calm a nightmare, or soothe an upset tummy and feel they have nothing left to give.

Help single parents to remember to take care of themselves, too. You love them, and you care about their well-being as much as their children. Remind them that they need to nourish their own bodies and spirits. Bring people around them to help, whether it's bringing meals, offering free babysitting, or help with transportation. Remind them that it's okay to ask for help—and to accept help—and that those offers are your hands and feet to love them.

In Jesus' name I pray, amen.

"But those who trust in the Lord will find new strength. They will soar high on wings like eagles. They will run and not grow weary. They will walk and not faint"
(Isa. 40:31).

Journal Your Thoughts

_____

_____

_____

_____

_____

_____

_____

_____

_____

_____

_____

_____

_____

_____

_____

_____

_____

_____

_____

_____

_____

_____

_____

_____

Day 209

Prayer for Empty Nesters

Dear Compassionate Father,

Change is difficult. This includes the change that comes after a couple has dedicated their lives to raising children only to find their homes empty again. The chaos of the children is gone, but the laughter is, too. Bedrooms and hallways are silent.

Be with these couples, Lord. Remind them that they are more than parents to their children. They are husbands and wives, friends and neighbors, and servants for you. Give these couples a vision for the life you have for them in this new season, whether that is serving more in their church, reaching out to their communities, or investing in relationships that they did not have time to do before.

Help these couples make good decisions. Help them invest in their marriages all along so that, when the children are gone, their bond remains strong. Remind them that they were a couple first, before the children came along. Once the children leave their home, it will be just the two of them again. Help them maintain their relationship as a priority so that their love for one another stays strong.

Give them wisdom in how to use their time and treasure. They have so many different things they can do now. Help them prioritize so that they invest in things that have lasting value to your kingdom.

In Jesus' name, amen.

"A person standing alone can be attacked and defeated, but two can stand back-to-back and conquer. Three are even better, for a triple-braided cord is not easily broken"
(Eccl. 4:12).

Journal Your Thoughts

Day 210

Prayer for Those Confused about Sexual Attraction and Orientation

Dear Heavenly Father,

This world can be confusing. Not only is the world broken and hurting, but we are broken and hurting inside, too. Even from birth, the sin that engulfs this world is at war with your perfect design for us. This comes out in many ways, including the confusion that many people have about their own sexual attraction and orientation.

You don't make broken vessels, God. Yet the pull toward the same sex or the rejection of someone's natural gender is often there from an early age. I don't understand how these things come to be, and it's not my job to figure them out. It's my job to love others, pray for them, and encourage them to look to you for the path they should take in life.

Help those struggling with this confusion to trust you. We live in a world that says, "Anything goes," and "If it feels good, do it." Give them the desire to live in a way that pleases you, even if it goes against their natural desires. Remind them that, no matter how much satisfaction the world may promise, those promises are empty. The only true and lasting peace comes from you.

I pray also for those who hate people with these issues. Same-sex attraction and rejection of natural gender are not your will, but neither is the hate that so many people express toward those who struggle in these areas. Remind those who hate that while one finger is pointing at someone else the other three are pointing back at them. We all need your grace, God. Let us point those who are struggling with these issues to you, and let us always do it in a spirit of love, knowing that we need your grace and forgiveness as much as they do.

In Jesus' name I pray, amen.

"And why worry about a speck in your friend's eye when you have a log in your own? How can you think of saying to your friend, 'Let me help you get rid of that speck in your eye,' when you can't see past the log in your own eye? Hypocrite! First get rid of the log in your own eye; then you will see well enough to deal with the speck in your friend's eye" (Matt. 7:3–5).

Journal Your Thoughts

Day 211

Prayer for Those Dealing with Change

Dear Precious Lord,

The only constant in this life is change. Just when we think we have it figured out, something happens to disrupt our plans and knock us off track.

It's easy to get frustrated, Lord. Most of us don't like change. We like to be in control. When things happen that are out of our control, we complain. We mutter under our breath. We complain to others. We complain to you. But it's in the times of change that you grow us the most. Whether it's change in our families, our finances, our health, or just seasons of life, it is during times of change that we learn to trust you more. When we cannot see the path ahead, we must trust your guiding hand. It is easy to say that we trust you, but it is when our lives are disrupted that we learn whether we really trust you or not.

Thank you, Jesus, that you are faithful. Even when we cannot understand or make sense of our circumstances, we can trust your character. We know that you love us. We know that you are wise and working for our good. Remind us of this when we grow fearful. Like Peter sinking into the sea, help us to keep our eyes on Jesus. We know that when we do, you will bring us safely through the storm.

In your precious name, amen.

"So Peter went over the side of the boat and walked on the water toward Jesus. But when he saw the strong wind and the waves, he was terrified and began to sink. 'Save me, Lord!' he shouted. Jesus immediately reached out

and grabbed him. 'You have so little faith,' Jesus said. 'Why did you doubt me?'" (Matt. 14:29–31).

Journal Your Thoughts

Topic Index

Prayers for the Mind

Prayers for Spiritual Growth

Prayers for Stronger Faith

Prayers for Self-Image

Prayers for Forgiveness and Repentance

Prayers for Our Words

About the Author

Dr. Emily A. Edwards is a gifted speaker, writer, and counselor whose compassion and insights have touched thousands of lives. Emily holds a Master's in Biblical Counseling from Victorious Christian Life Institute and earned her Ph.D. in Christian Counseling from Vision International University. She is a Licensed Clinical Pastoral Counselor and the author of multiple books, including *Ready & Waiting: A Biblical Approach to Singleness, Dating, and Preparation for Marriage* (book and companion workbook), *What's Your Problem? Discovering God's Greatness in the Midst of Your Storms* (book and companion workbook), *Grace Letters: Practical Steps to Experiencing Transformation Through Forgiveness*, and co-author of *Table Grace: Practical Steps to Escaping the Cycle of Rejection*. Her passion is bringing healing and wholeness to those who have experienced the pain of loneliness, rejection, and sorrow.

Made in the USA
Middletown, DE
01 May 2025

74973369R00262